The Straight Line

POETS ON POETRY

David Lehman, General Editor
Donald Hall, Founding Editor

New titles

Tess Gallagher, *Soul Barnacles*
Rachel Hadas, *Merrill, Cavafy, Poems, and Dreams*
Ron Padgett, *The Straight Line*
Charles Simic, *A Fly in the Soup*

Recently published

Edward Hirsch, *Responsive Reading*
John Koethe, *Poetry at One Remove*
Yusef Komunyakaa, *Blue Notes*
Philip Larkin, *Required Writing*
Alicia Suskin Ostriker, *Dancing at the Devil's Party*
James Tate, *The Route as Briefed*

Also available are collections by

A. R. Ammons, Robert Bly, Philip Booth, Marianne Boruch,
Hayden Carruth, Fred Chappell, Amy Clampitt, Tom Clark,
Douglas Crase, Robert Creeley, Donald Davie, Peter Davison,
Tess Gallagher, Suzanne Gardinier, Allen Grossman, Thom Gunn,
John Haines, Donald Hall, Joy Harjo, Robert Hayden,
Daniel Hoffman, Jonathan Holden, John Hollander,
Andrew Hudgins, Josephine Jacobsen, Weldon Kees,
Galway Kinnell, Mary Kinzie, Kenneth Koch, Richard Kostelanetz,
Maxine Kumin, Martin Lammon (editor), David Lehman,
Philip Levine, John Logan, William Logan, William Matthews,
William Meredith, Jane Miller, Carol Muske, John Frederick Nims,
Geoffrey O'Brien, Gregory Orr, Marge Piercy, Anne Sexton,
Charles Simic, Louis Simpson, William Stafford, Anne Stevenson,
May Swenson, Richard Tillinghast, Diane Wakoski, C. K. Williams,
Alan Williamson, Charles Wright, and James Wright

Ron Padgett

The Straight Line

WRITINGS ON POETRY AND POETS

Ann Arbor

THE UNIVERSITY OF MICHIGAN PRESS

This book is for George Schneeman.

Copyright © Ron Padgett 2000
All rights reserved
Published in the United States of America by
The University of Michigan Press
Manufactured in the United States of America
♾ Printed on acid-free paper

2003   2002   2001   2000   4   3   2   1

*A CIP catalog record for this book is available
from the British Library.*

Library of Congress Cataloging-in-Publication Data

Padgett, Ron.
   The straight line : writings on poetry and poets /
Ron Padgett.
      p. cm. — (Poets on poetry)
   ISBN 0-472-09726-1 (cloth : alk. paper)
   ISBN 0-472-06726-5 (pbk. : alk. paper)
   1. Poetics—Poetry.   2. Creative writing—Study and
teaching.   3. Poetics.   4. Poetry.   I. Title.   II. Series.

PS3566.A32 A6 2000
811′54—dc21   00-033803

Acknowledgments

Grateful acknowledgment is made to the following publishers for permission to reprint previously published materials. "Yak and Yak," "Haiku," "Poem" ("Funny . . ."), "Poetic License," "Voice," "Talking to Vladimir Mayakovsky," "Louisiana Perch," "First Drift," "Euphues," "Who and Each," and "Essay on Imagination" from *New & Selected Poems* by Ron Padgett, reprinted by permission of David R. Godine, Publisher, Inc., copyright © 1995 by Ron Padgett. "16 November 1964" and "Joe Brainard's Painting *Bingo*" from *Great Balls of Fire* by Ron Padgett, reprinted by permission of Coffee House Press, copyright © 1990 by Ron Padgett. "Gimmicks" from *The Whole Word Catalogue 2,* edited by Bill Zavatsky and Ron Padgett, copyright © 1977 by Teachers & Writers Collaborative and reprinted by permission of Teachers & Writers Collaborative. Poetic forms essays from *The Teachers & Writers Handbook of Poetic Forms,* edited by Ron Padgett, copyright © 1987 by Teachers & Writers Collaborative and reprinted by permission of Teachers & Writers Collaborative. Every effort has been made to trace the ownership of all copyrighted material in this book and to obtain permission for its use.

A Note on the Title

I seem to remember reading—or did I dream it?—a college mathematics textbook that defined the straight line as a series of imaginary points that do not change direction. In my mind's eye, a straight line is a visible thing, and therefore this definition appealed to me because it suggested that a real thing could be made wholly of imaginary parts. A possible literary corollary came to mind, that the poetic line is a real thing made of imaginary parts. I also like the colloquial undertones of *straight* (direct) and *line* (information), as in a 1930s American film in which a gambler leans toward his tout and says, "Gimme the straight line." The pieces collected in this volume attempt, in their own curvy and sometimes oblique ways, to give an honest response to that gambler; that is, to you, the reader.

—R. P.

Contents

Yak and Yak

I am saying
that grammar is the direct result of how humans feel in the
    world;
or rather,
that grammar follows from what we experience viscerally and
punctuation keeps it that way;
that for instance, people walking down the street
are forming various sentences with their bodies,
and as the schoolgirl turns the corner the meaning
changes, oh so natural. Just so the wind
that suddenly turns the corner has just blown your hair off!
You go indoors and write,
"The wind has blown my hair away,"
then shift your weight and add, "almost."
For in your mind your arms have stretched to catch your
    head,
in which Pig Latin is understood but Dog not.
"Omecay erehay, etlay emay elltay ouyay omethingsay atthay
    ouyay ughtoay otay owknay."
In Hawaiian countries there was a battle over there,
anyhow, and when she heard the racket and the battle
of the fierce pineapples clashing under a warm moon,
she wrote across the sky, with her magic finger,
in glowing light, that she would not love her man anymore.
The palm trees stood like so many silent exclamation points
in the flowing beat of the night's heart.

16 November 1964

As this morning seemed special when I woke up
I decided, as is my custom, to go for a refreshing walk
In the street. Preparing myself for the unexpected, I
Combed my hair and generally made ready. I was ready.
In the hall outside my door the lady from down the hall
Shouted my name to get my attention. I waited
As she came down the hall with a newspaper in her hand.
I expected the worst. On the other hand, one can never tell
What mystery might spring up from the most commonplace,
For example, the lady and her newspaper. She wanted
To show me a headline which must have disturbed her,
Because her hands trembled as she read to me, "FIREMEN
   CHOP
THEIR WAY THROUGH SHED." I thanked the lady
And started toward the stairs when I realized that
The headline she had read me was rather astonishing.
I went back inside and wrote it down. Then down

In the street a suspicious-looking fellow approached me
And gave me a handbill, which, had not one of its words
Caught my eye, would have been quickly disposed of.
The word was "they"; it appeared once in the sentence,
"Do you realize that *they* are undermining your existence?"
I was puzzled by the fact that the word *they* should be
   italicized,
And the more I thought about it, the more it fascinated me.
Now, I have a small blue notebook which I carry with me
At all times, in case of any emergencies,
Such as the one I have just mentioned. I opened my book
To "T" and wrote down the word.
Well, my walk hadn't gotten along very far until

I remembered how close to the park I live, and how rarely
I go there. So picking up my stride and finally passing
A handsome girl, I reached the stone wall which bounds the
    park.
Ah, the red park! Where as a child I remember I had
Done so many things. . . . But that was in the dim past. . . .
Right in the middle of my reveries I felt someone
Looking at me and, turning, I was face to face with a very old
    man,

Who, without saying one word, gave me a small white card
With hands on it. Underneath the rows of hands
The card read: "I AM A DEAF MUTE. I SELL THIS CARD TO MAKE
    A LIVING. COULD YOU HELP? THANK YOU."
The old man did not take his eyes
Off me as I fished around in my pocket, and even after
I had dropped some coins into his limp hand, he stood there
Looking at me. How embarrassing it is when someone
    watches you
Put your hand into your pocket!
The old man finally shuffled away with my second donation.
I don't know why, but I was so upset that I had to sit down.
I disregarded the rain that never seemed to go away
From that bench, because I was so upset. A few moments
Later my senses came back to me and I found a small white
    card
In my hands, and its curious rows. Then I remembered
That their language is called "finger talk." The thought
Of talking fingers, so to speak, so thrilled me that the words
"Finger talk" went into my notebook, under "they."
    "Who knows,"
I said to myself, "by the end of the day I may have written a
    poem!"
"Now is no time to worry about poetry," my stomach chided
    me,
And I made my way out of the park, generally enjoying
    the air.

At one of the numerous lunch counters which dot our city
I ordered my lunch. The place was busy with people in a
    hurry,

And I knew I would have to wait for my order to arrive,
    and then
It would probably be the wrong thing or cold. To pass
    the time
I glanced through the two-page menu, which bore
On the title page the word "MENU."
Then it was that what had been happening to me all day,
This sudden illumination of the trivial, happened again.
Menu! How mundane, yet how miraculous! I wrote it down,
Under "M." It made my fourth entry, and I hoped for many
    more,
Since I had a great desire to write a long, beautiful poem,
Though I have nothing against short poems. But sometimes
I feel as if short poems are sort of a hoax, don't you?
Well, to get on, I finished the lunch, which was not
So bad as I had anticipated, and I once again met the air

With a light step. My next step? Who knows! I was full of
    vim! Vinegar!
It so happened that a young mother was strolling her little
    daughter
And that a small book dropped from the mother's handbag.
I went to fetch the book with every intention of returning
It to its proper owner, when I noticed the title and began
To think about it. The title was "THE PLUM, THE PRUNE, AND
    THE APRICOT."
Had this story once held me enchanted as a child? The last
Sentence seemed so familiar: "Forbidden pleasures leave a
    bitter taste."
It was all I could do to keep myself from bursting into tears,
And only the thought of recording this sentence, so
    mysterious
In its familiarity, prevented me from doing just that.
I slipped the book into my pocket, like a long-lost memento.
The experiences of this day, so exciting and wonderful,
    were still
Rather tiring, so I went into a theater to see a movie
    and to rest
My eyes. The movie was very boring and I soon left.

Back in my apartment I managed a small dinner, in.
  "TV DINNER."
Began to attract me, but when I went to write it down I
  hesitated:
The modern poet must be discriminating.

So now I sit in the kitchen writing in you, diary, a soda bottle
In my hand. "You are like me, soda bottle," I just said,
Shaking it and making it fizz. There must be something in a
  soda bottle
That we can understand, though I don't know what. Just as
  there must be
Something of value, to someone, in my blue notebook. I
  open my book
To see the four lines I have written down during the day, in
  those spare moments of inspiration:

> *This offers us the stale air of the balcony*
> *Of the future which you don't want or can,*
> *Blue, marigolds, the sum of all that you love in him,*
> *Where is it?*

Joe Brainard's Painting *Bingo*

I suffer when I sit next to Joe Brainard's painting *Bingo*

I could have made that line into a whole stanza

I suffer
When I sit
Next to Joe
Brainard's painting
Bingo

Or I could change the line arrangement

I suffer when I sit

That sounds like hemorrhoids
I don't know anything about hemorrhoids
Such as if it hurts to sit when you have them
If so I must not have them
Because it doesn't hurt me to sit
I probably sit about 8/15 of my life

Also I don't suffer
When I sit next to Joe Brainard

Actually I don't even suffer
When I sit next to his painting *Bingo*
Or for that matter any of his paintings

In fact I didn't originally say
I suffer when I sit next to Joe Brainard's painting *Bingo*
My wife said it
In response to something I had said
About another painting of his
She had misunderstood what I had said

Lettera

Old typewriter,
when my Olympia got stolen
and I went to Europe
I found you
in the Galeries Lafayette,
with your French keyboard,
accent marks and Italian name:
and never thought of you in terms of olives
until tonight, lying in bed,
vague unregistered thises and thats
flitting through my head the way
my words have flitted through you
and out, and I thought back
to that Smith-Corona, used,
the executive office-model Olympia,
and its sidekick the big black ancient monster
with keys I had to bang and its table tipped
over bending the keys sideways
with the impact: my greatest poem!
Then, leaving them behind and buying a portable
    Olympia on upper Broadway,
the one thieves stole
just before we sailed
and I've had you ever since,
through thick and thin,
changed a lot of ribbons, always black,
threading the inky cloth into its grooves,
cleaning and oiling the mechanism,
leaving you idle for months and then feeling
your soft touch again

Song

Learning to write,
be a good person and get to heaven
are all the same thing,

but trying to do them all at once
is enough to drive you crazy

Poem

I'm in the house.
It's nice out: warm
sun on cold snow.
First day of spring
or last of winter.
My legs run down
the stairs and out
the door, my top
half here typing

Talking to Vladimir Mayakovsky

All right, I admit it:
    It was just a dream I had last night.
      I was trudging along a muddy path
in a column of downcast men
    on the blackened outskirts of New York,
      the twilight dingy and ruined,
the future without hope
    as we marched along
      in our soiled, proletariat rags.
To my left was Mayakovsky, head shaved,
    and next to him his friend
      with gray beard and dark cap.
"You've got to admit," Mayakovsky
    was saying, "that this is a pretty good
      way to write a poem."
"Yes," I said, "the momentum
    is sustained by our walking forward,
      the desolate landscape seeps into every word,
and you're free to say anything you want."
    "That's because we're inside the poem,"
      he said, "not outside." Puddles
of oily water gleamed dully beneath the low clouds.
    "That's why my poems were so big:
      there's more room *inside*."
The hard line of his jaw flexed and
    the men dispersed. I followed
      his friend behind a wall
to hear the poem go on
    in the lecture the friend was giving on history,
      but no, the real poem had finished.
I went back to the spot
    where the poem had finished.
      Vladimir had left the poem.

Haiku

First: five syllables
Second: seven syllables
Third: five syllables

Poem

Funny, I hear
Frank O'Hara's
voice tonight
in my head—
e.g. when I
think in words
he's saying them
or his tone
is in them.
I'm glad
I heard him
when he was alive
and I'm glad I can
hear him now
and not be sorry,
just have it all here,
the way Jimmy, stark
naked with rose petals
stuck to his body,
said, "Have you seen
Frank? I heard
he's in town tonight."

Voice

I have always laughed
when someone spoke of a young writer
"finding his voice." I took it
literally: had he lost his voice?
Had he thrown it and had it
not returned? Or perhaps they
were referring to his newspaper
the *Village Voice*? He's trying
to find his *Voice.*
      What isn't
funny is that so many young writers
seem to have found this notion
credible: they set off in search
of their voice, as if it were
a single thing, a treasure
difficult to find but worth
the effort. I never thought
such a thing existed. Until
recently. Now I know it does.
I hope I never find mine. I
wish to remain a phony the rest of my life.

Louisiana Perch

Certain words disappear from a language:
their meanings become attenuated,
grow antique, insanely remote or small,
vanish.

           Or become something else:
transport. Mack
the truck driver falls for a waitress
    where the water flows. The

great words are those without meaning:
      from   a   their   or
      Or   the   for   a   the
      The   those

The rest are fragile, transitory
like the waitress, a

beautiful slender young girl!
I love her! Want to
marry her! Have hamburgers!
Have hamburgers! Have hamburgers!

Tennyson Invincible

Where is the poem "Tennyson Invincible"
I've been wanting to write for almost two years?
It seems to exist
in a world continuous but not contiguous
with mine
like an alternative to an event:
I ate a larger bowl of cereal
this morning and wasn't killed by that speeding taxi!
Inside the taxi a passenger stares
glumly into the future
which the past absorbs as he
leads his life through it.
Pretty soon poof
No Nothing. A thousand
years pass. An animal
with a shiny white ball for a head
declames, through strange body vibrations,
"Tennyson Invincible." This
of course will not happen—
just a fantasy I had.

First Drift

The writing of poems
and the living of life
seem to require
paying hard attention
to any and everything,
and experiencing
a kind of mental orgasm.
Yikes! Do I
mean that?
Unfortunately, I'm afraid
I did, dipped to scoop
an idea from the roadside,
the mental roadside that runs
alongside the mental highway
that leads to a mental hospital.
I have never been a patient
in a mental hospital, because
I think it would be an extremely bad place to be.
So I stay out.
And stay home.
And go down the street,
looking intently at everything.
Sometimes the people in the street
laugh and turn into sheet music
torn from the sky and left to flutter down
into the metaphor that hides behind the deity,
and will not show itself,
like a basement beneath the ocean,
with a tree that grew through a sheet of glass
on which your face was painted,
like a clown's, in the early morning

when it was just starting to rain
and the animals are moving, and the tents
are rippling in the breeze, and inside Glenda
the chimpanzee is completing a quadruple somersault
from shining bar to shining bar.

Euphues

I dunno about this *Euphues.*
Lyly's language is gorgeous,
of course, occasionally irritating,
too, so you feel satisfied
to have the experience just
behind you. You get up and go outside
and have a hot dog in the sunlight and
think about the conjunctions,
those pinions
that allow our sentences to rotate in mid-course:
"The afternoon was mild, although not yet over,"
placing the dependent clause in direct opposition
to the main clause, like a woman who suddenly
turns to face you and it takes
your breath away—there is a moment
of silence and intensity—the boats
are frozen on the bay and no little doggie barks.
    "I've been meaning to say something to you . . . ,"
she begins. And your heart
sinks: something massive
is about to happen,
you will be joined to this woman
with a tremendous force, something like
gravity, in which
hats float down onto our heads and we smile.
    We smile toward this Countess of Pembroke
with her delicate lips and translation
of *The Psalms* with her brother Sir Philip Sydney,
the great poet and of the great tradition of
fine comportment. His conjunctions
were in perfect order
and he exuded a harmony,
a tone actually heard in the air.

Olivetti Lettera

Goodbye, little Lettera.
It was nice with you again.
I once loved a girl and oh
Well I once loved a girl.

You are so small, the way
what I remember is
packed into my human skull
and it's dark in there.

And it's singing in there,
this typewriter who is a
girl, then, an Italian girl,
undressing, slowly, in the dark.

Who and Each

I got up early Sunday morning
because it occurred to me that the word
which
might have come from a combination of *who* and *each*
and reached for the *OED*
which for me
(I think of it not
as the *Oxford English Dictionary*
but as the *O Erat Demonstrandum*)
has the last word:
"Hwelc, huelc, hwaelc, huaelc, huoelc, hwaelc, wheche, weche,
whech, qwech, queche, qheche, qwel, quelk, hwilc, wilc, hwilch,
wilch, whilc, whillc, whilk, whylke, whilke, whilk, wilke, whylk,
whilk, quilc, quilke, qwilk, quylk, quhylk, quilk, quhilk, hwic,
wic, hwich, wyche, wich, hwych, wiche, whiche, whyche, wych,
whych, which, quiche, quyche, quich, quych, qwiche, qwych,
qwyche, quhich, hwylc, hwulch, hulch, wulc, whulc, wulch,
whulche": Teutonic belching.

But in little tiny type: "For the compounds *gewilc,
aeghwilc,* see *Each.*"
Now, if you want to talk *belching.* . . .
It was raining outside
with the blue-gray hiss of tires
against the wet street
I would soon walk my dog in,
the street I drove an airplane up
earlier this morning in a dream
in which the Latin word *quisque* appeared to me,
as if it meant *each which*
in the sea of *eisdem, quicumque,* and *uterque.*
Thus I spend my days,
waiting for my friends to die.

Essay on Imagination

So I go to the baseball stadium. It is large, larger than I had thought it would be, and it is surprisingly fast, moving along at about forty miles per hour. At this rate we will be playing Saint Louis by morning! By a stroke of good fortune, I happen to be the only person on the promenade deck, a real treat. The smooth green expanse of field before me is, for this moment, all mine. Am I dreaming, I ask myself. The answer is no, you are not dreaming, you are having a fantasy that you are at a baseball stadium that is also an ocean liner. The answer makes me slump deeper into my personality, the part I sleep in, and so I get sleepy. If I go to sleep, I can dream about the ball field, and what might have happened there as we crossed the ocean, me and the blond girl who has just arrived, wearing black shorts that are cut achingly high in the back and a black bandanna across her chest, and as she mounts the stairs with a drowsy rolling of her hips I realize that she is a composite of all the girls I've ever glimpsed in the street with that pang of fleeting lust that glows for a moment and fades away into me and then rolls back out, because the power of the imagination cannot be contained, no matter how hard we try.

Poetic License

This license certifies
That Ron Padgett may tell whatever lies
His heart desires
Until it expires

PROSE WORKS

Problems with Words

Although a grapefruit looks nothing like a grape and a pineapple has nothing to do with either a pine or an apple, I always knew perfectly well what those fruits were. I had grown up eating them at home. But at a certain point—in my early twenties, I think—I began having trouble discriminating between the words *pineapple* and *grapefruit.*

When the actual fruits were before me, I had no trouble. But in conversation I was mysteriously unable to differentiate between them. "Honey, at the store why don't you pick up a fresh grapefruit, to go with the ham." Wife: "A grapefruit? You mean *pineapple,* don't you?" So I began simply to guess: the odds were that I would be right half the time. The other half I pretended was one of those perfectly ordinary slips of the tongue: "How silly of me, of course I meant *pineapple.*" Eventually I began to dread using those two words at all. One day, after ten years of confusion, my wife said, "You have trouble with those words, don't you?"

The simplest solution, which I used for a while, was to avoid using them. I would look up the road of a particular sentence and see one of those words approaching, then I would veer off onto a service road and go around it, using some clever circumlocution. This mental agility pleased me privately but also caused me to wonder about my problem.

Now, seeing those words up ahead in a sentence, I no longer veer away, I arbitrarily pick one of them and call up a mental picture of it. After a moment the picture appears, something like a dictionary illustration. Then I match the picture with the place the word is to occupy in the approaching syntactical slot: if it matches up, I go ahead and say it; if it

From *Blood Work* (Bamberger Books, 1993).

doesn't, I automatically say the other word. As I say the word, a little smile comes to my lips and I laugh inwardly at what a strange person I am and how peculiar it is that someone supposedly so articulate should have to resort to such a clunky mechanism, just to say "grapefruit" or "pineapple."

I've always had trouble with the word *atavism*. I can never remember what it means, no matter how often I look it up in the dictionary, and its context never seems to provide a clue to its meaning. Its Latin root was one I never came across, so I can't decipher it etymologically. Furthermore, I can never invent quite the right mnemonic device for it.

Instead, as soon as my eye hits the word, I freeze. Then I tell myself to relax and think about it for a moment, just let my mind go: surely its meaning will come to me. I begin to free-associate. In my mind's eye I see a large jungle clearing, at night, with a group of indigenous people hopping up and down in front of a bonfire dedicated to the carved image of their deity, a totem pole with pointed head and almond eyes that curve upwards at the outer points. The muffled gutteral growl of their tribal chant goes out into the darkness around them. Their blood sacrifice is being delayed because they have no victim, *yet*. Will they see me?

I open my eyes. In my hands I am still holding the book. I reread the sentence in question, projecting my fantasy onto the word *atavistic*. It never fits, so I look it up in the dictionary and then reread the sentence, which makes perfect sense. Within ten minutes its meaning begins to fade again.

Foreign Language

Our concept of "foreign" language seems somewhat misplaced when you consider that we Americans think we speak and write English, when in fact we speak and write an offshoot of English that probably should be called American. It seems to me that the differences between the two languages are more remarkable than the similarities: British tradition, intonation, vocabulary, and sense of form are alien to all but the highly educated American. Good British writing is often more ordered, more exact, and more decorous than American writing, whereas ours is frequently braver and more colorful. English is a language foreign to most Americans, just as the dialect spoken on the Dutch islands of Friesland, despite its remarkable similarity to English, is foreign to Britishers; as Black American dialect is foreign to much of the rest of American society; as deep southern dialects are gibberish to the native of Cape Cod. One's idea of "foreign" depends on one's location, geographical and otherwise; and what I'm suggesting here, to give perspective to one's local point of view, is a global point of view, not because it is fashionable but because it is healthy and humane.

When I was growing up, in the limited cultural atmosphere of blue-collar Oklahoma in the 1940s and 1950s, I used to laugh when I heard someone speaking a foreign language, especially an Asian one. To me foreign languages sounded "funny," in both senses of the word. Others thought they sounded funny in only the sense of odd or peculiar. In other words, *not like us.* I think my seeing foreign languages as both

---

"Foreign Language" was a talk given at the Detroit Institute of Arts as part of its Lines poetry series curated by George Tysh in 1981 and published in *Blood Work* (Bamberger Books, 1993).

odd and amusing helped save me from this jingoist fate. I had a corollary taste for Pig Latin and for nonsense talk, and I was always amazed how an ordinary word gradually loses its meaning when repeated aloud over and over. Car car car car car car car car car car car car car car car car car car car car car car. An insane crow flying over a traffic jam in a primitive religious ritual!

My sense of language was also broadened by comedians such as Jerry Lewis, Red Skelton, and Jonathan Winters, with their voice changes, and Milton Berle with his bad puns, and George Burns, with his wittily restrained remarks, and a host of others. These were the poets of my childhood, because they made language itself attractive, dynamic, and surprising. I enjoyed their foreignness: most comedians of the time seemed to be Jewish and from either New York or Philadelphia. My mother had been born to Ozark farmers in a log house in Mountain Home, Arkansas, where there was no dearth of humor or color, but of diversity. So, born with a twang in my heart, I grew up with a Brooklynese residue in my head, via the comedians. I liked it that they were different from me, and I admired them. Maybe that's why, in my early teens, I loved Latin and the language of plane geometry: axiom, hypotenuse, trapezoid, corollary, parallelogram, perpendicular, theorem, rhombus. There is a particularity of sonority to the vocabulary of any specialized discipline that is similar to the particularity of sonority to a foreign language.

Aside from English, the only other language I have concentrated on at any appreciable length is French. Now, even without knowing French, you know that it has its own sound, that the "music" of French is different from the "music" of English. The unexpected bonus is that, once you have heard the music of another language, you hear so much more clearly and fully the music of your own.

Which leads us to the question: whose language? We have been made aware, and none too soon, of the social implications of sexism in language. As Orwell and others have pointed out, there are political implications, too. Those who wish to manipulate a society find it necessary to manipulate that society's language, to make it as restricted and/or meaningless as possible. To take an obvious example: if the news media are censored or state controlled (as Tass was in the former Soviet Union), their language becomes a powerful instrument of control. In the United States we have a subtler form of this, self-control, and I doubt that we get a much fuller or better idea of the world from our own small-minded news media than the Soviets did from theirs. But in order not to be reduced to the picture the media give us, we can, with another language or two, get the picture from other points of view. Read *Le Monde,* for example, for another picture of the world, perhaps no better or worse a picture than that of the *New York Times* or of *Pravda* but at least one that reminds us that other views exist, that there is a complexity and multiplicity to "truth" that Americans don't seem to want to remember.

Our government has shown little interest in encouraging its people to learn foreign languages. Did a recent ten-year decline in foreign language instruction in our country augur a new political climate (i.e., "We're Americans, we're right, and we're not interested in what the rest of the world thinks"), or does it reflect the proliferation of English as the language of international business and diplomacy, or both, or what? I don't know. I do know that, if we allow ourselves to drift passively along with the linguistic jingoism that restricts us to our own language and our own culture and our own literature, then that language and that culture and that literature will be diminished, and we will have done ourselves a disservice. It's up to us as individuals to take off these cultural (and therefore political and spiritual) blinders and see what is out there in the world.

In terms of language, there are any number of ways to do this. Simply studying the vocabulary of languages that have fed into English can give us a sense of the history of those words individually and that vocabulary in general. It's a truism, one worth repeating every once in a while, that words are born, they grow and change, they travel, and they die. Being aware of the histories and properties of the words we use is a part of standard good craftsmanship, just as a good carpenter knows the history and properties of various woods: you would not build a spring-box out of pine, nor would you floor a living room with hemlock. Of course, this applies more directly to the study of one's own language than to the study of a foreign language, but it should be kept in mind that the distance between, say, English and French was not always what it is today: at one time French was the language of the English court, where a strange blend of vocabularies and accents must have taken place, something like contemporary New York City, where sometimes you gotta shlepp down to the bodega for some chow mein.

One thing a foreign vocabulary gives you is the culture it's part of. There are objects, games, tools, foods, actions, jokes, techniques, and so forth that have names in one language but not in another. A good way of bringing oneself closer to that culture is to learn its words for things. Some words are quite similar (such as *air* in English and *l'air* in French), but mousse au chocolat is *not* chocolate pudding. The French finally got around to seeing what a weekend is, but of course they had no word for it, so they called it "le weekend." Cultural attitudes come through clearly in such untranslatable words, and by defining a foreign culture they also redefine our own.

Until now I've talked mostly about the meaning and sounds of words. But what about the way they look? I became aware that the look of a page of poetry could affect its sound and sense when I first read e. e. cummings, whose typography and white space were as important as his message and his music. All readers are affected, subtly or not, by the look of the page. When I read a text in French, I feel a little different, because, although the words use virtually the same alphabet as ours do, they are arranged in particularly French patterns determined by French rules, so that suddenly a line of poetry will burst with, say, *e*'s. (Or, to take a more obvious example, imagine a page of Italian with no *o*'s!) Also affecting the look are the wonderful accent marks, the grave and acute accents pointing fore and aft, the tickling cedilla, the child's-idea-of-a-rooftop circumflex. Who can resist the tilde and the umlaut? Not to mention the other worlds of arabic script and Chinese calligraphy.

Like meaning, sound, and look, the syntax and grammar of a foreign language will permit things to be said in that language that can't be said in English. (It works the other way around, too, of course.) You cannot read two supposedly similar books such as *A la recherche du temps perdu* and *Look Homeward, Angel* and not be struck even more forcibly by the differences in syntactical structures of language. The flow of words is a tributary to an even greater flow, that of the history of the intelligent energy of an entire culture. I'm thinking, for some reason, of the Age of Reason, and of Descartes in particular, and how the new thinking must have gone hand in hand with a new sense of the role of conjunctions, especially the *although-whereas-moreover* type, conjunctions that must have taken on a greater importance in a mentality that valued discrimination, order, and system. I don't really know if Descartes used those particular words any more or any better than, say, Montaigne, but I would guess that they weren't quite the same words for him.

Adjacent to this line of thinking is the matter of gender in language, which I skirted before. Compared to the romance languages, English has relatively little gender, notably in its nouns. All romance language nouns have genders, which is one of the reasons Americans tend to find them difficult. Gender in language brings up some intriguing questions. It seems appropriate that words for "woman" and "girl" should be feminine, and it's not too hard to understand why words for house (*la maison*), room (*la chambre*), car (*la voiture*), and so on should be feminine, but it is very difficult to understand the justification, other than by a simple claim to tradition, for the genders of words such as *table, cloud,* or *future.* And it seems to me that a major cultural decision was made at some point when the word *esprit* was identified as masculine.

Although I wouldn't assume that a language is superior or inferior simply on the basis of its complexity, I think it's safe to say that languages with more highly inflected nouns—in this case those with gender—are richer in structure, since gender permits a more periodic sentence, with antecedents at a far greater distance from their referents. Even *it* in romance languages can have gender, so you don't have to repeat the noun itself for clarification. Another possibility consists in using gender to set up suggestive resonances between things. For instance, in French you can mention "la pluie" (feminine noun meaning "rain") in a sentence, with a man there. And you can begin the next sentence with *elle* (meaning "it," the rain). This example probably muddies the general point I'm trying to make, but I like the way it sounds aloud, and it makes me think of the possibility of love between this man and the rain, a he and a sort of she. This associative thinking is precisely the kind of interesting result of cross-referencing one's English (where gender is sexual) and another language (such as French, where it is not necessarily). That is, what started as pedantic speculation led me directly into an imagined rural scene with a man ambling along in the soft summer rain.

At this point I'm going to try to describe an interesting mental process that sometimes takes place during translation. Perhaps an anecdote and some examples will help introduce this elusive subject. In the spring of 1963 I tried the literary experiment of intentional mistranslation. That is, I took a French text—in this case some early poems by Pierre Reverdy—and translated them as though I knew only a few words of French and had to make dunderheaded phonetic guesses as to the others. For example, the original line "Elle passe devant la bouche d'égout" came out "El Paso invents the bush of gout." Questions of quality aside, this rather odd procedure resulted in an inspired lunacy: a woman going past becomes the town of El Paso, Texas, the preposition *devant* becomes the word *invents*, "la bouche d'égout" a "bush of gout." (Now that I think about it, a sewer hole is not all that different from a bush of gout.) As I careened through six such poems, my mind became like a Ping-Pong ball knocked back and forth between the two languages in an echo chamber, each word resonating with its connotations and the strange interweaving of nonsense between the two language tracks. It was an exhilarating and only slightly spooky experience. Not long afterward I decided to add the other dimension—namely, "straight" translations—to the original and the mistranslation. That was when I realized that a similar mental process takes place during traditional translation, but set, of course, in a more conventional context, and therefore more controlled, requiring a focusing of those echoes rather than an excited scattering of them.

In doing these and other mistranslations, I had no idea I was influencing my "own" writing. I thought I was simply making forays into a magic territory that might at any moment disappear in a puff of smoke. But a change was taking place in my attitude toward language, accelerated by the disorientation of mistranslation. This disorientation enabled me to produce an enormous amount of bad poetry, but it also detonated some of the mental patterns that were in fact holding me back. At least that's my understanding of the experience. Being both skeptic and optimist, I'm not sure I wouldn't have been better off leaving the old brain synapses as they were, but I don't have any regrets at seeing some of my conventional notions of language blown to bits. After the smoke had cleared and the nouns and verbs could be seen scurrying about confused in an alien landscape, a desire for order reasserted itself, and later I returned to conventional syntax feeling refreshed and amiable, free to follow tradition now that I no longer felt stifled by it. I should add that these observations are all in retrospect: I didn't sit around saying to myself, "Now I will return to conventional syntax and feel free to follow tradition."

These are some of the more technical and abstruse reasons for getting involved with a foreign language. The step beyond this involvement is translation, something like going from dating to marriage. And while that step may drive you bats, it has several virtues.

First, it's a marvelous way to read. To translate someone's work, you eventually have to read it slowly and closely, the very opposite of speed reading. You have to read the text at something closer to the speed at which it was written, to let it breathe at its own rate. Your spirit hovers like a carbon copy over the original spirit. At this reduced speed your reading takes on a different character, because you are able to concentrate on details better. It's comparable to the difference between speeding along a road and walking along the same road. Suddenly you see that the ditch is fringed with clover, or that Apollinaire has let himself stack up rows of prepositional phrases in one of his stories. Or that some of John Ashbery's poetry uses conjunctions as hinges. Or that some lines get their grace from a certain kind of "soft" noun. Or that there's a feeling in the poem you never noticed before, a feeling that mingles with the surface feeling and creates a mysterious wealth in the feeling of the whole.

Another thing I like about translating is that I do it the way I used to do homework, in a fairly concerted, serious, but relaxing frame of mind. I fall in love with my beautiful new notebooks, brought back from Paris like holy relics, which I fill with my black ink scrawl. Soon the very sight of them on my desk makes me feel warm and inspired, as though what one writes actually does do some good for the universe. And I'm proud of my effort to listen carefully to a fellow writer, to bend my ear to his lips, just me and Jean-Jacques Rousseau!

Let me add one final reason for translating: you might produce something beautiful: the flower of the entire process. You might produce something that can be held up to the light and that will shed its own beautiful radiance on the world, independent of you.

Four French Poets
and the Cubist Painters

From around 1910 to around 1918 in Paris, the interaction of painters and poets helped create an extraordinary new art. The best modernist French poets of the time were involved with "The New Spirit" in literature and visual art—which included artists as varied as Modigliani, Chagall, and the Delaunays— but they were particularly involved with the Cubist painters. This involvement helped create a more powerful and beautiful visual art on the one side and a more powerful and beautiful literature on the other. Nowadays, the term *Cubist painting* is a part of art history, whereas *Cubist poetry* is hardly ever heard. And for a good reason: it probably doesn't exist.

When asked about "la poésie cubiste," Pierre Reverdy, the poet closest to the Cubist painters and the most profound aesthetician of Cubism, replied, "A ridiculous term!" He was right. The poetry one is tempted to label "Cubist" owes too much to other aesthetics, such as Simultaneism, to suit such a tag.

There was much, though, in the poetry of Reverdy, Guillaume Apollinaire, Blaise Cendrars, and Max Jacob that could be described as Cubist. Their work contained a multiplicity of viewpoints (different planes in the same poem) and shifting voices (on the same plane). Their poetry exemplified the same play on appearance and reality as did Cubist collage: use of found materials and trompe l'oeil—is it a newspaper clipping

---

"Four French Poets and the Cubist Painters" was a talk given at Franklin Furnace in New York, to complement its 1983 "Cubist Prints / Cubist Books" exhibition, organized by Donna Stein. It was published in the exhibition catalog, which doubled as an issue of *Flue* magazine (vol. 4, nos. 1–2 [Fall 1983]).

or a painting of one?—and play on words, which might be described as "trompe l'esprit." The poets' new and sometimes fragmented syntactical arrangements were similar to the juxtaposition of objects in Cubist art. With Reverdy, in particular, the subject matter and the treatment of it were those of the Cubists: everyday objects and occurrences (including dreams) rendered with a subdued palette. Add all this to the fact that many of the poets and Cubist painters were living in the same neighborhood, some in the same building and even the same room, and, at one point, in the same poverty, and you have the basis for the aesthetic sympathy that helped make the best Cubist art so profound, lyrical, and continually fresh.

These qualities are easily accessible in their visual form: Cubist imagery has become part of an international language. You don't have to speak French to appreciate this art. The same qualities are not so accessible in the poetry, because it usually requires translation, a step away from the original (and sometimes a step in the wrong direction). And so, although the stature of the work of Braque and Reverdy is comparable, one is well known and the other is not. What I hope will be evident in the brief selections of the following four poets is that the New Spirit that was moving in Cubist painting was also moving in the poetry of the writers nearest to Cubism.

Guillaume Apollinaire was by far the most effective champion of Cubism. His book *The Cubist Painters* (1913) made a resounding announcement to the world that the new art had arrived and was to be taken into serious account. Writing art criticism to make a living, he was also creating his own extraordinary art, in poems such as "Lundi rue Christine":

Monday Rue Christine

The concierge's mother and the concierge will let anybody in
If you're a man you'll go with me tonight
All we need is one guy to watch the main door
While the other one goes up

Three lit gas jets
The boss has tuberculosis
When you're finished we'll play a game of backgammon
An orchestra conductor with a sore throat
When you come to Tunis I'll see to it you smoke some weed

That rings a bell

Piles of saucers some flowers a calendar
Bam bam bam
Hell I owe 300 francs to my landlady
And I'd rather chop it right off than pay her

I leave at 8:27
Six mirrors look back and forth at themselves forever
I think it's going to get even more confused
Dear Sir
You are a crummy pimp
That lady holds more food than a garbage can
Louise forgot her fur
Well I don't even have a fur and I'm not cold
The Dane smokes his cigarette over a timetable
The black cat crosses the bar

Those crêpes were marvelous
The fountain runs
Dress black as her fingernails
It's completely impossible
Here you are sir
The malachite ring
The floor is strewn with sawdust
So it's true
The red-headed waitress ran away with the bookseller

A newspaperman I know only very slightly

Listen James I have something very serious to say to you

Passengers and cargo

He says to me, Sir, would you care to see what I can do in the
    way of etchings and paintings?
I have just a small maid

After lunch Café du Luxembourg

Once there he introduces me to this big fat guy
Who says,
Listen, it's charming
In Smyrna in Naples in Tunis
But damn it where is that
The last time I was in China
Eight or nine years ago
Honor often depends on what time of day it is
The major fifth

The poet seems to be sitting in a cafe, transcribing whatever strikes his eye and ear, but his technique, rather than closing down the space, opens it up. We are made to feel the multiplicity of the situation, the quickness and largeness of the world, as we are also in his masterpiece "Zone" and in "The Windows," written, according to legend, at the studio of Robert Delaunay.

The Windows

From red to green all the yellow dies
When the macaws sing in their native forests
Pihi brought down
There is a poem to be written about this bird that has only
    one wing
We'll wire it across town
Giant traumatism
It makes your eyes water
Look there's a pretty girl among the young girls from Turin
The poor young man blew his nose on his white tie
You will raise the curtain
And now look the window is opening
Spiders when hands wove the light
Beauty paleness unfathomable violets
We'll try to get some rest but won't be able to
Beginning at midnight
When you have time you are free
Periwinkles Monkfish multiple Sunflowers and the Sea Urchin
    of the sun going down
An old pair of yellow shoes in front of the window
Towers
The towers they're the streets
Wells
Wells they're the squares
Wells
Hollow trees which shelter vagabond Capresses
The Octoroons are singing songs so beautiful you want to die
To their chestnut-colored girls
And the goose honk-honk trumpets in the north
Where raccoon hunters
Are scraping their pelts
Twinkling diamond
Vancouver

> Where the train white with snow and night lights flees from
> winter
> O Paris
> From red to green all the yellow dies
> Paris Vancouver Thenburg Nowsville New York and the
> Antilles
> The window is opening like an orange
> The beautiful fruit of light

To some degree, Apollinaire was doing for the window what Braque and Picasso were doing for the guitar and the fruit bowl.

The poems that Max Jacob wrote during this period—particularly the prose poems in his masterpiece *The Dice Cup*—demonstrate a sense of multiplicity that is oddly comic and oddly convincing:

Alas!

I am the spitting image of my grandfather: same narrow shoulders, same mean words. Why two copies of the same man?

In the following poem, a great deal happens within a small frame, as if a novella had been compressed into a single paragraph.

Adventure Novel

Well, it's true! There I was, like Philoctetes! Abandoned by the boat on an unknown crag because my foot hurt. The terrible thing is that my pants were ripped off by the sea! Got the information. I am nowhere else but on the shores of modest England. "Surely I will soon find a policeman!" That's what came up, a policeman, and one who spoke French. "You don't recognize me," he said in that language, "I'm the husband of your English maid!" There was a reason I didn't recognize him, it's that I never had an English maid. Hiding my nudity as good as ill with some foliage, he took me to a neighboring town and to a tailor there. And when I wanted to pay, "Never mind," he said, "secret police funds," or "polite funds," I didn't understand the word very well.

Of course none of this is "true," and this is not a novella. Things aren't what they seem.

The binding has some golden grillwork which imprisons cocka-
toos of a thousand colors, boats with sails made of postage
stamps, sultans with bird of paradise feathers on their heads to
show how very rich they are. The book imprisons heroines who
are very poor, steamboats which are very black, and poor gray
sparrows. The author is a head imprisoned by a big white wall
(I am alluding to his starched shirtfront).

My Life

The town to take is in a room. The enemy's plunder isn't heavy
and the enemy doesn't even take it away because he doesn't
need any money since it's a story and only a story. The town has
ramparts of painted wood: we'll cut them out and glue them on
our book. There are two chapters or parts. Here is a red king
with a gold crown riding a saw: that's chapter 2. I don't remem-
ber chapter 1 any more.

In this kind of art, you don't really need chapter 1. "It was
the Cubist goal," Jacob wrote in 1922, "to arrive at the real by
nonrealist means." Jacob's quick juxtapositions of tone, like
the juxtapositions of planes in Cubist painting, are in the ser-
vice of an art that does not represent things, it *presents* them.

Like Apollinaire and Jacob, Blaise Cendrars wrote poetry in
different styles and forms, but the poetry he wrote just before
World War I is his most cubistic. Like the Cubist collagists,
Cendrars incorporated the newspaper into his work:

News Flash

OKLAHOMA, *January 20, 1914*
Three prisoners get hold of revolvers
They kill their guard and grab the prison keys
They come running out of their cells and kill four guards in
    the yard
Then they grab the young prison secretary
And get into a carriage waiting for them at the gate
They leave at top speed
While guards fire their revolvers in the direction of the
    fugitives

A few guards jump on horses and ride in pursuit of the
    convicts
Both sides exchange shots
The young girl is wounded by a shot fired by one of the
    guards

A bullet shoots down the horse pulling the carriage
The guards can move in
They find the prisoners dead their bodies riddled with bullets
Mr. Thomas, former member of Congress who was visiting
    the prison,
Congratulates the girl

Copied telegram-poem in *Paris-Midi*

Cendrars makes no attempt to disguise his source, including
even the dateline. By placing the story in a new context—that
of art instead of journalism—he has changed both story and
context far more radically than he did by slightly revising the
original newspaper article.

Two other poems from the same collection (*Nineteen Elastic
Poems*) demonstrate Cendrars's literary affinity with Cubism:

Still Lifes

For Roger de la Fresnaye

Green
The fast trot of the artillerymen passes over the geometry
I strip down
Soon I'd be nothing but steel
Without the square rule of the light
Yellow
Bugle of modernity
The American filing cabinet
Is as dry and
Cool
As the first fields are green
Normandy
And the architect's table
Is as strictly beautiful
Black
With a bottle of India ink

And some blue shirts
Blue
Red
So there's also a liter, a liter of sensuality
And that latest style
White
Sheets of white paper

(April 1914)

The Head

The guillotine is the masterpiece of plastic art
Its click
Creates perpetual motion
Everyone knows about Christopher Columbus's egg
Which was a flat egg, a stationary egg, the egg of an inventor
Archipenko's sculpture is the first ovoidal egg
Held in intense equilibrium
Like an immobile top
On its animated point
Speed
It throws off
Multicolored waves
Colored zones
And turns in depth
Nude.
New.
Total.

(July 1914)

The idea of stripping things of all ornament, of getting down to the most basic and fundamental form, is one that recurs often in Pierre Reverdy's writings on literature and art, and the art he wrote about was usually that of Braque, Picasso, Gris, or Henri Laurens. In an interview, Reverdy said, "From 1910 to 1914 I learned the Cubist's lesson. The paintings, so stripped down, so simple! . . . I wanted to get that in literature." Using a monochromatic verbal palette, he wrote haunting and beautiful poems, poems that, given a casual reading, seem so bare that they hardly exist. On closer reading, though, they reveal a depth and strength that are comparable to the best in Cubist painting. (Reverdy was not, however, given to writing "anthology pieces," so he doesn't shine forth particularly well in brief selections.) One untitled little prose poem has always reminded me of the poverty many artists and writers of that time shared:

> Back then coal had
> become as precious
> and rare as gold
> nuggets and I wrote
> in an attic where
> the snow falling
> through cracks in
> the roof turned
> blue

Aside from its shape and trimness, however, this poem isn't particularly suggestive of Cubism. The following poem, with its quick synthesis, is:

Mao-Tcha

> The scar lives
> The box closes
> Between the lips
> A nest
> of pearls
> A smiling portrait
> the mirror
> Where the window shines
> A live fish
> In its cage
> free
> The water rushes out
> The Chinese run
> on the tapestry

In a more typical and spiritual vein is this poem from his collection *Les Epaves du ciel* (*Flotsam from the Sky*):

Sun

> Someone has just gone
> And in the room
> A sigh is left

<pre>
        Life deserted
          The street
                                And the open window
        A sunbeam
        On the green lawn
</pre>

Much of Reverdy's poetry during this period was written ei-
ther in block (prose) format or in staggered lines (as in "Sun")
in which the disposition of words on the page, like Cubist
planes, is as integral to the poem as are its vocabulary and
syntax.

It is odd that, in spite of all the affinities between poets and
Cubists, there were so few direct collaborations. More often
than not the artist would contribute a frontispiece drawing for
a book or the poet would provide a poem for an exhibition
catalogue. One of the few exceptions is Reverdy's collabora-
tion with Gris, *Au Soleil du Plafond* (*The Ceiling Sun*). The origi-
nal project called for twenty poems by Reverdy to match
twenty lithographs by Gris, each with a one-to-one relation-
ship. Reverdy completed his twenty poems and Gris eleven of
his images, at which point Gris broke with his dealer, who had
commissioned the project. Later Reverdy and Gris quarreled,
and then Gris died, leaving the project unrealized. In 1947,
when Gris's former dealer died, the originals were rediscov-
ered and in 1955 issued under Reverdy's supervision. What a
gorgeous piece of work it is! The poems, deceptively simple to
read (and maddeningly hard to translate) are a perfect coun-
terpart to the visual images. Here is one example:

Coffee Mill

On the tablecloth there's a little dust or some coffee grounds.
War or peacefulness on the foreheads that wrinkle together.
The smell mixed with the cries of the evening, they all close
their eyes and the mill has its dark daily grind, like our heads.
In the circle of voices a cloud rises. A windowpane at the lip
that grinds our thoughts.

How fitting that the poet closest to the Cubist painters
should have found the term *Cubist poetry* to be "ridiculous!"
For, even though Reverdy, Cendrars, Jacob, and Apollinaire

were not part of a Cubist poetry movement, they were an essential part of the way Cubism happened, not only by promoting it, defending it, and to some degree legitimizing it, and not only by providing the personal support that only a colleague and friend can give, but also by exchanging points of view with the painters—poet as painter and painter as poet—which lent to both a multiplicity that was also fundamental to the art they created.

Blaise et Moi

Why this impertinent title?

Because I feel as if I know him, as if he were my great-uncle, as if we were buddies.

Because I can hear his voice in my ear, and he addresses me as *tu*.

By the time I was twenty, I had read a few of Blaise Cendrars's poems in translation and in French anthologies, but they had left no particular impression on me. He was just another French poet. It wasn't until a few years later, when I moved to Paris, that I began to get the feel of this particular French poet. And it was through his prose.

Living on a small scholarship, I entertained myself by reading inexpensive paperbacks in my hotel room at night. So it was that I read Cendrars's novels in the Livre de Poche series, beginning with *L'Or*, through *Moravigine*, to *Bourlinguer*. I only half-understood them, but for the first time I began to read French without translating it in my head, and I grew to like the voice I heard in these stories, off-the-cuff and down-to-earth, the voice of a raconteur.

Not long afterward an editor of the *Paris Review* asked me to translate some Cendrars poems to accompany an interview with him. So I read the complete poetry and was dazzled by its diversity and captivated by the freshness of *Kodak* and *Feuilles de route*. This wonderful discovery led me to the rest of his work.

As an American I was flattered by his interest in my country, and especially in the state I had grown up in, Oklahoma.

"Blaise et Moi" was given as a talk at a meeting of the Blaise Cendrars International Society in 1983. It was published in the organization's newsletter, *Feuille de routes*.

There it was: his books on Hollywood and Al Capone, the American settings of *Kodak,* the Oklahoma setting of his poem "News Flash," and his translation of the autobiography of Oklahoma outlaw Al Jennings. Also he had written "Easter in New York" in the city I had been living in since I left Oklahoma. And now I was writing poetry in his city. For me the exchange was powerful.

But Cendrars is not the kind of poet that vast numbers of American poets get really close to. I think I can explain why I am an exception by quoting an autobiographical sketch I wrote a few years ago, in response to the question "Why did you become a poet?" (I probably should have given Cendrars's response to the same question: "Because.")

In the United States there are thousands of people who write poetry but who, because of doubt or modesty, do not call themselves poets. They think of themselves as doctors, journalists, teachers, housewives, etc. Their poetry may be bad or mediocre or even better than that of those who call themselves poets, but that's not the question here. What interests me is that there are some who call themselves poets and others who don't. I find myself among those who do.

At various times I have asked myself why. The responses to that question still don't satisfy me, but I'll repeat them here, while admitting that for me the whole subject remains cloudy.

One of the reasons is that being a poet involves the beauty of mystery—a debatable notion, I know.

Another, less debatable reason is the influence of my father. He never had the slightest artistic pretension. For him poetry, and all the so-called pure arts, came from Mars. His father's suicide after a poker game left my grandmother, a simple country girl, with three young children, no money, in Oklahoma, in the middle of the Great Depression. My father was ten years old. Like his older brother, he had to earn money for the family. Life was hard. But it made him tough and self-sufficient, the kind of guy who could tell society to go to hell, because deep in his heart he believed that society was partially responsible for his situation.

During the Second World War, at the age of eighteen, he worked in a gas station. He had been refused by the army because of an "unstable nervous condition," but the story in our family was that he had broken his leg in a motorcycle accident. In fact such an accident did occur but *after* his refusal by the draft. In any case, pumping gas didn't pay very well, and in 1942 or 1943 he started selling his clients an additional liquid: whiskey. I should point out that until 1959 the sale of alcohol was illegal in Oklahoma, even wine. But for him selling hooch wasn't any different than selling gas, except that hooch was more lucrative. After six months he quit pumping gas and became a full-time bootlegger.

Over the years his clients included the mayor, the chief of police, and many officers whom he had known since childhood—most of the cops and crooks came from the same blue-collar neighborhood. And so an interesting situation developed: my father became a respected and likable outlaw but a criminal just the same.

Some were not amused: the upstanding citizens, the respectable types, the Baptists, etc. And, from the age of seven or eight, I began to sense the disdain of some of their children. Even certain teachers looked at me in a curious way that I did not understand. Although I was a model student, smarter than most of my classmates, and like an average American boy I played baseball, etc., deep down I bore the social stigma of my father and his profession. He was somewhat legendary in our city. Good for him but not so good for me, even though I admired the strength of his spirit, his flair, and the myth he represented. For me his heroism was simultaneously admirable and painful.

One day, at the age of sixteen, I told myself two things. First, I would never be a soldier. Never. Second, to the question "What am I?" I answered, "I am a poet. Forever." And here I am!

I should add that nineteen years later I understand that my image of the poet (as outlaw) was stale, dating from nineteenth-century romanticism, but it was one that formed me.

Of course, there are other reasons that I became a poet: my passion for comic books (as a child, I read very few books, but I read tons of comic books); meeting other "outlaw" intellectuals (we formed a small band apart); having English teachers who praised my poems (they dubbed them "magnificent"); and other reasons that I have never even imagined.

But I believe the fundamental reason remains the example set by my father, who continues to think that poetry is something from the planet Mars but that if his son is a poet, it must be a good planet. In fact, when he finally got around to asking me what I was going to do with my life, and I answered "Be a poet," he thought for a moment, and said, "Well, okay." When I was going away to college and in a sense leaving home, he gave me only one bit of advice: "Stay out of jail."

Be free!

So Blaise and I have in common this sympathy for the unfettered individual, the underdog, the outlaw, the vagabond, the tough but lovable lone wolves of this world, although neither he nor I could be described as all of these. We both love our own quirky, personal scholarship, but we could not be described as scholars in the usual sense. We both have a taste for the eccentric and even the bizarre, though there is nothing very eccentric or bizarre about either of us. We are both quick to see the legendary in the everyday. We love the tradition of Rimbaud and Whitman, though with a little humor thrown in.

In mentioning myself in the same breath as these writers, I do not mean to imply that my work is comparable to theirs. But in another sense I do put myself in their company: I choose to spend my time with poets such as Cendrars, reading him, thinking about him, translating him, and living with him as a part of my daily life. He allows—even invites—us to do that. And what better company could we want?

Pierre's Room

In Narbonne, I drive straight to the Novelty, a cheap hotel French truck drivers like. I get a room without bath for fourteen dollars. In the hotel bar, the *patron* is talking to a regular. I interrupt them to ask if they know the best way to Moussoulens ("Moo-soo-lahn"). They look puzzled.

"Oh, you mean 'Moo-soo-linz,' " says the *patron*. His name is Claude Strazzera. He looks grumpy, with a pencil mustache.

"Yes, I'm looking for the farmhouse where the poet Pierre Reverdy lived."

He gives me directions on how to get to Moussoulens. Sort of go-left-then-right-then-left-then-left-then-right-you-can't-miss-it. I repeat his instructions and head out to the car, but just as I open the car door, M. Strazzera comes running out and waves me back in. Something's wrong.

He and the regular are having a discussion.

"Moussoulens is a place name," the regular keeps saying, "not the name of a village." It's just a spot. No houses. Do I really want to go there? We'd better check.

M. Strazzera grabs the phone and calls somebody downtown. He has friends. "Moussoulens, the home of Narbonnais poet Pierre Reverdy. . . ."

"You know," the regular says to me, "there's another Moussoulens."

Huh.

"And it's a village, not just a place name. It's over near Carcassonne, though. Could that be the place?"

"I don't know. All I know is that the farm was called *la Borio de Blanc*."

"Pierre Reverdy—did you read his novel about Tahiti?"

From *Blood Work* (Bamberger Books, 1993).

"About Haiti?"

"No, Tahiti. He wrote a wonderful novel about Tahiti. He was a doctor."

"Pierre Reverdy? No, I don't think he was a doctor. He worked as a proofreader in Paris. And I don't think he ever published a novel about Tahiti."

"Then it's another Pierre Reverdy. The Pierre Reverdy I'm talking about was a doctor here in Narbonne. I know people he treated."

"Is that a common name here?"

"No, but it's not uncommon, either. There are some Reverdys here today."

M. Strazzera is now phoning the police station for more information. Meanwhile, the afternoon is wearing on, and I am starting to fear that it will get dark before I can get to this Moussoulens.

"Try Carcassonne," suggests the regular.

M. Strazzera dials Information, then City Hall in Carcassonne.

"Yes," he reports, "there is a Moussoulens outside of Carcassonne."

"I told you so," says the regular.

Maybe there was a second Pierre Reverdy, too.

"But was it the Moussoulens where Pierre Reverdy lived?" asks M. Strazzera. Then he says, "I've got an idea. We'll call the library. They know everything."

He calls the library. "This is Claude Strazzera, Hôtel Novelty. I have a tourist here."

As he talks, a phrase pops into my mind: "*Au pied de la Montage Noire. . . .*" I say it out loud.

"Aha!" says the regular. "If it's at the foot of the Black Mountain, then it has to be the Moussoulens outside of Carcassonne."

M. Strazzera hangs up. He has the look of a hunter who has just put a bullet between the eyes of a grizzly bear.

"We're in luck. At the library, they're having an exhibition devoted to the life of Pierre Reverdy, to celebrate the centenary of his birth. He was from Narbonne, you know. The librarian says for you to come see it—the library will be open for two more hours, and you can walk there—and also to go upstairs and ask for M. Viala, in the Municipal Archives. He has done a lot of research on Reverdy and will help you find whatever you need."

The truth is that I just want to get into the car and drive out to the family farm, but I have no choice now. "It's only a five-minute walk," he adds.

The Bibliothèque Municipale is on the rue Jean-Jaurès, and M. Viala's office is on the top floor. His door is open. I poke my head in and give a little knock. He looks up from his desk. He has a long mustache and wears a tweed jacket, one of those fellows who acts older than he is. He's maybe forty. There is a pleasant smell of honey tobacco lingering in the air of his office, with its low ceiling and old, comfortable atmosphere. He smiles, shakes my hand, and launches into telling me what he has discovered about Pierre Reverdy in the municipal archives.

"Reverdy was born on Friday the thirteenth, but he was very superstitious, so he always gave his date of birth as September eleventh," he says, leading me downstairs to the exhibition cases.

"Here's a picture of the house he was born in, 3 boulevard du Collège, now called boulevard Marcel Sembat. And here's the house he lived in as a young child, 1 rue de l'Ancienne Mairie, now called rue Benjamin Crémieux. Here's his birth certificate. He was delivered by a midwife. Notice that the mother's name is listed on it as 'unknown.' The father is listed as 'Henri Pierre Reverdy,' which was Pierre's name, also. Notice that his father did not recognize him legally until Pierre was six years old. And his mother did not recognize him legally until he was twenty. See here: her name was Jean Rose Esclopié. And here's his military record. On this questionnaire, he said he had no experience shooting guns, riding horses, etc. He answered *no* to every question! Here you see he was 4-F because of a heart condition."

"Oh, so he wasn't discharged?"

"No, he wasn't inducted."

The other display cases contain photographs of Reverdy and copies of his books, most of which I have seen. A few readers, mostly young people, glance up at us. We seem important because we are allowed to talk out loud.

"But about Moussoulens: come back up to my office when you've looked at the exhibition." And off he goes.

I take a few photos of the display cases and, using a close-up lens, of some of the documents. Then I wait a respectable amount of time before going back up to M. Viala's office.

He picks up the phone and calls the Municipal Archives in Carcassonne. His counterpart there confirms that yes, the Reverdy family farm was in Moussoulens, outside of Carcassonne. M. Viala goes out and comes back with a detailed map of the Aude region, and there it is, Moussoulens, a little dot.

But now it is too late in the day to drive there, so I say thank you and goodbye, and go out for a walk, to see the birthplace and childhood house. I go first to the rue Benjamin Crémieux, but can't find a number 1. There seem to be only two numbers, something like 13 and 17. I ask several passersby, but they don't know. Ah, there's a bookstore on the corner. But they don't know either. All they know is that there's a plaque that's going to be put up to honor Reverdy. They read about it in the newspaper.

So I set off for the house he was born in. It's a longer walk, but the afternoon is pleasant, with some leaves drifting down across the slanting sunlight. And there, in the block after the school the street was once named after, is the building Pierre was born in, September 13, 1889, exactly one hundred years and fifty days ago.

But it's just another building, three or four stories, gray stone, another French building, with cars parked in front. I try to recreate the scene of a hundred years ago, but I don't know which floor to use in my imagination. The "unknown" mother, the stunning news that Pierre was a bastard, the vague relationship of father to mother—it all swirls around in my mind, erasing my visual fantasies as soon as I conjure them. I need a cup of coffee.

The next morning, after breakfast and many thank-you's, I drive to Carcassonne, get a room, and head toward Moussoulens, which is only ten or fifteen minutes outside of town and easily found with a detailed Michelin map.

It appears to be a sleepy little village, but the sleep is even deeper today, which is All Saints' Day. Everything is closed except the bakery, where I go in and ask the young woman for directions to la Borio de Blanc, the Reverdy family farm about eighty years ago. She's new in these parts herself, but maybe M. Fiche, across the street, could tell me: his family has lived here for generations, and he used to be town secretary.

I go across the street and tap at the glass door. Inside, a man lifts himself out of an easy chair and pads toward me in his socks.

"I'm sorry to bother you. I'm looking for the Reverdy family farm, la Borio de Blanc, and the girl in the bakery told me you might be able to help."

"*Certainement,*" he says, rolling the *r*. He has the same accent as Reverdy, the same dark hair, but he seems more congenial than Reverdy was supposed to have been. "You just go down this street until you get to the monument, then turn left. That road will take you right to the farm. It's only about five hundred yards outside of town. The present owner is named Loisel, Mme. Loisel."

His directions take me out to a farmhouse, but at first I'm not sure that this is la Borio de Blanc. A man is backing out in a car.

"Excuse me, is this la Borio de Blanc, the old Reverdy farm?"

"I don't know," he answers pleasantly, "I'm just visiting. Ask inside."

With some hesitation—though not much, since I've come this far—I crunch across the gravel and ring the doorbell. In a few moments a woman opens the door. She looks handsome and intelligent, with dark hair and brown eyes.

"I'm sorry to bother you, but I'm a tourist, an American tourist, a poet, actually, and I'm trying to find the farm where the poet Pierre Reverdy lived."

"This is it," she smiles. "Would you like to come in and look around?"

"Uh, well, I don't want to bother you. . . ."

"But it would be no bother at all."

"Really? That's wonderful!"

Inside, I introduce myself formally to Mme. Loisel. She tells me the farm has been in the family since her father bought it more than fifty years ago. The basic structure is the same as when Reverdy lived here, except for the living room, which has been enlarged by the removal of a wall that partitioned off two small rooms, to the left and right as you enter. And of course the interior has been modernized: new floors, new kitchen, new bathroom fixtures, all in good taste. The attached barn has been converted to living space. (In fact, the Loisels, members of the *gîtes ruraux* system, rent out that space to guests, such as the gentleman in the car I had spoken to outside.) The main structure is a long, two-story stone building with a red tile roof. Upstairs, off a hallway, are the bedrooms. The first one on the left is Pierre's, the one he used when he was home from school on vacations.

We peer into the room. It's about eight by twelve feet, but I almost can't see it, because I keep thinking, "Little Pierre fell asleep here, in *this* room." At the far end is a single window, looking out on the front side of the house, with a view of trees, fields, and the sky. In the wall to the left is a small doorway that used to lead into the hayloft. I can almost hear the hay. The animals shift in their stalls—or do they? Probably only a cow or two, maybe some rabbits and chickens outside, since this farm was primarily a vineyard. And still is. Now the room belongs to Mme. Loisel's little boy.

"Sometimes he slept in the room next door, his parents' room," she says. We take a look, but it doesn't have the same radiance. She gestures vaguely to the bathroom further down the hall.

We go downstairs and out the back door. The red and yellow and green vines that stretch all the way up to the village seem to crackle pleasantly in the autumn light pouring down from the pure blue sky. A deliciously cool breeze causes a huge pine to sough softly above us.

"Was that tree here when Pierre lived here?"

"Almost certainly. There were several others, one over here and another over there, but they had to be taken down when they were blown over in a storm."

A man in wading boots and gentleman farmer clothes comes out of the house.

"This is my husband," says Mme. Loisel.

We smile and say hello.

"I'm just doing some work around the place," he explains.

"Oh," I say, "I just realized that it's a holiday and I'm taking up all your time."

"No, not at all, really," says Mme. Loisel.

"These vineyards are so beautiful," I say. "Are the property lines still the same?"

"Yes," says Mme. Loisel. She points out the boundaries. "They grew the grapes here, harvested them, pressed them— did everything. Come, we'll show you the old vats."

In a big shed just beyond the house, we view the vats. It's possible that the Loisels, perhaps the French in general, have a feeling for wine vats that we Americans do not have. Sensing my blankness, Mme. Loisel says, "Why don't you take a walk down to the orchard? My husband will show you where Pierre tied his donkey to one of the trees: you can still see the ring it made around the trunk. And the bulge in the tree he used as a bench."

"Yes," says M. Loisel, "I'm just going down to spray the trees now. Would you like to come along?"

Mme. Loisel goes back inside the house and I stroll with M. Loisel down a typically beautiful allée of plane trees, maybe two hundred feet long. On the right, about halfway down, is the tree with the bulge, about seat high, and higher up, the ring that grew because Pierre tied his donkey there. The tree is dying, but M. Loisel is doing everything he can to save it. The vineyards are to the right, and to the left is a stream, with a sluice that once powered a grain mill. Straight ahead is the orchard. As he goes on ahead to spray his trees, M. Loisel tells me to take my time and look all around. I walk over to the stream and find the old sluice gate, now rusted, and I look back up through the trees, where the leaves are shaking and glimmering gently against the bright blue sky. It's as pretty a day as possible.

When I finally mosey back up to the house, a polite teenage girl—Mme. Loisel's daughter—tells me that her mother has gone into town, and that she'll be right back. I stroll around outside for a while, waiting for *madame* to return. I can't just leave. When finally she drives up and gets out of the car, I see that she has not only done some shopping, but she has also dressed up. Complete with earrings.

"This has been wonderful, this visit," I begin.

"But you must come inside and have a drink with us," she insists.

"Well, just a tiny one," I say.

In the living room, we're joined by M. Loisel again, and *madame* offers us a choice of drinks. We choose a local specialty, an apertif that tastes like a rich port wine. Whatever its name, it goes down smooth and easy. She stands up and goes to each of us with a little tray of snacks. I choose the dried apple chips, which go nicely with the drink. She even serves her husband, who after the second round tells her, very politely, "*Non, merci beaucoup.*" It's been a long time since I've seen anyone play the role of perfect hostess. It's like Tulsa in the 1950s.

"My father had owned this place for a few years, when a man knocked at the door and said that he used to live here. It was Reverdy. He had a woman with him, but never introduced her. He asked if he could look around. My father invited him in. Pierre ran from room to room, excited like a kid, and he walked down the allée, looked at the old tree, and asked for a glass of wine from the vineyard."

Whatever she had served me is working its wonders. I am feeling warm and pleasantly vague.

"Then he left and never came back. And he never introduced the woman. But from what my father later learned, it must have been Coco Chanel."

"Yes," I say, "Reverdy and Chanel were . . . friends."

M. and Mme. Loisel smile at my choice of words.

"It must have been Coco Chanel," she says. "She was petite and wearing black."

"I suppose the village was pretty sleepy back then," I suggest. "It seems awfully quiet now."

"Oh," smiles Mme. Loisel impishly, "it's quiet on the surface, but underneath. . . ." She waves her hands around, pantomiming turbulence. "The people will smile and act as if everything is fine, but then suddenly they explode."

"Like Reverdy, no? He had an explosive temper."

"Yes."

"A sort of Spanish temperament? It goes with his rolling *r*'s."

"Just like me," says Mme. Loisel. "I'm sure I have Catalan

blood, as do many people in this area." She starts to talk about the history of the region, the Cathars, and the area between Carcassonne and the Pyrenees. Both she and her husband are well educated. I wonder what they do for a living.

"What does *la Borio de Blanc* mean, exactly?" I ask.

"*Borio* is an old Provençal word that means *place* or *area*," she explains. "Blanc was the name of the man who owned the farm before the Reverdys. La Borio de Blanc: Blanc's Place. But actually the farm is better known as *la Jonquerolle.*"

"And Reverdy's wife," says M. Loisel, "do you know about her?"

"I think she's dead now."

"Really?" says Mme. Loisel, surprised. "We saw her just a few years ago."

"Oh," I say. "I said that only because I saw a portrait of Pierre that she had given to the Fondation Maeght in 1975, so I assumed it was a bequest."

"No, we saw her two years ago, in Solesmes," says *madame*. "But we didn't speak to her. What could we say? That we live in the house Pierre grew up in? And then what? But you, you love Reverdy—you should go to Solesmes and meet her."

"I will, if I can muster the courage," I say. But I am only being polite. The plans for my trip don't include Solesmes.

The talk shifts to Pierre's books and books about him. A few years ago a local writer had published a little book about Reverdy's childhood. And here is a picture of the place as it used to look. She hands me a book opened to an illustration.

"I bought this book in 1965," I say, "and you have no idea how many times I've looked at this picture and wondered about this place. In fact, I must tell you that being here is, for me, incredible, it's overwhelming." Perhaps the drink has enabled me to say what I feel at the moment. "And your hospitality has been wonderful."

"But it is our pleasure," they both reply. Their gentility seems authentic: for them this is the normal way to behave.

"Thank you. And now I must be going. It's two o'clock!" And with that we say goodbye. When I open the car door, I glance back up at the window of Pierre's room. How happy he must have been here.

I spend the rest of the day and that night in Carcassonne. The trip continues as planned: exploring the areas around Cahors and Sarlat, then on to Angoulême to drop the car off and get the train to Paris. In Angoulême the train station and car rental agency are both in the Place de la Gare, as is a recommended hotel.

I park in the square, buy a ticket for tomorrow's train, and then am told by the ticket clerk that there might be rail strike. Tomorrow. So, after some thought, I cash in the ticket, notify the car agency that I'm keeping the car, and head north. Maybe I'll spend the night in Tours.

But Tours isn't that far from Le Mans, and Le Mans isn't that far from Solesmes. The landscape flattens as I blast along the superhighway. At Château du Loir I take a smaller road through Vaas, le Lude, la Flèche, and Sablé, and suddenly I find myself entering Solesmes and immediately exiting, it's so small. I turn around and go back.

There's no tourist information center. There's almost no one on the street. I stop at the building that houses both the town hall and the post office. The town hall is closed Monday afternoons, but in the little post office I find a young woman behind its only window, serving a monk in a brown robe unloading packages and letters from a golden cart. He's from the Benedictine abbey, the Abbaye Saint-Pierre, one of the best-known centers of Gregorian chant studies in the world. He takes a long time with his numerous transactions, fumbling about in an old coin purse for those last twenty centimes of what amounted to around four hundred dollars' postage. Finally it's my turn.

"Hello. I need some information. I'm looking for the house where the poet Pierre Reverdy lived."

"I don't know," she answers, "but maybe this gentleman can help you."

I turn to the monk. He has close-cropped gray hair, wire-rimmed glasses, rounded features, lively eyes, intense and secretly funny. Maybe it has something to do with the fact that he keeps one foot in each of two different worlds. In any case, his face has a glow different from any I have seen on this trip.

I explain that I am an American admirer of Pierre Reverdy's

poetry. He asks me where I am staying, and when I say I don't know yet—I've just arrived—he tells me that Mme. Reverdy can't put me up. I nearly leap out of my shoes telling him that I had expected nothing of the sort, that I wouldn't even knock on her door or speak to her. He seems reassured, but he keeps looking deeply into my eyes. I wonder what he sees.

"Come with me," he says, "I'll show you the house."

We walk half a block toward the abbey, and at the corner he turns and points down the street. "It's the last house on the right. She comes to Vespers every day. But please don't bother her, she's quite old, and looking rather drawn lately."

"She *must* be old."

"Yes. Would you like to visit his tomb, too? You just go down this street about two blocks. It's on the right."

"Thank you very much."

He smiles and says goodbye, turning away with his little cart.

At the cemetery, I walk down row after row of graves, looking for the tomb. Some of the stones don't even have names on them. Then I spy a man across the way. He seems to be a florist, or perhaps the caretaker. I outwait my hesitation and go over to ask him if he knows where the grave is. Yes, the grave is here somewhere, he's sure, but where? He is solicitous and eager to help. After some random searching, he notices a young priest who has wandered in and asks him for help. Yes, the grave is here somewhere, the young priest smiles, and he thinks it's . . . somewhere. We all wander around a bit. Suddenly the man calls out, "*Voilà!*"

When I thank him for his help, he says, "That's okay. I spend a lot of time here. I lost my wife eighteen months ago." He and the young priest drift off.

I look down at the slab. It's red marble, low and flat, with specks of black and gray in it. Lying on top of it, also flat, is a black cross, and slanting across the bottom of the cross is a black bar with the word MAGNIFICAT. Along the front edge of the marble—only three or four inches thick—the words HENRI PIERRE REVERDY 1889–1960, flush right. The left half must be reserved for his wife Henriette. Henri, Henriette.

I quickly take some photos—the 4 P.M. autumn light is beautiful, but waning—and then I stand there, looking down at the grave, and I get the curious idea that I'm much *taller* than Pierre. I feel as if I'm looking down at his stone from a height of eight or nine feet, not six feet two. I try to imagine him in the coffin but get only a general sense of morbidness, so I abandon that line of thinking.

I drive to the parking lot across the street from his house. A lot of new houses have been built since he moved here in 1926, and the abbey's growing reputation must have put Solesmes on the map. Solesmes feels less remote than it must have in the 1920s.

Through the windshield I take some photos of the house, and I decide to wait until Henriette comes out.

As I sit there in the car, gazing at the garden wall and the top half of the house, I remember a dream. At a small seaside village in France, I get off the train and walk a few hundred yards toward the beach, where Reverdy's cottage looks out over the water. No one is home. Inside, it is quiet, cool, clean, refreshingly pretty but not decorative. I am feeling hesitant about barging in, when his wife enters and says pleasantly (and she was supposed to be sour and cranky), "Pierre's out now, but I expect him back soon." At that moment he comes in the front door and greets me. He suggests we go out to lunch at a nearby restaurant he likes.

It is austere in a way that tells me it's a good restaurant. The dishes Pierre ordered arrive, one after the other, until the entire table is covered. The word *cassoulet* suddenly takes on a fierce pleasure. Across the table, Pierre eats with calm sobriety. To my left, my son is undecided as to what to drink. The waitress is growing restive: "*Comme boisson?*" "What do you want? Coke? Milk? What?" I prod him. The waitress starts off across the room. "*De l'eau*," I call out to her. "*Ce n'est qu'un gosse,*" she says. "Brat is more like it," I answer in English. "Oh, it's not that bad," she chides me. Suddenly I realize that Pierre has selected this restaurant because the waitresses are English.

It is now 2:30 in the afternoon, but the light has grown dim. Pierre is in deep shadow, with only a circular patch of brightness on his white shirtfront. Otherwise I can't see him, but he seems to be either asleep or in deep thought.

He is sitting in the chair to my right, with a sheet of white paper and an ink pen, the old kind with a nib, and he is writing furiously. I recognize his handwriting and realize that he is writing a poem. I move to the chair opposite him and, on a sheet of paper of my own, start writing a poem in two-line stanzas that describe him writing. When we finish our poems, we stand up. He smiles.

"What did you write?" he asks pleasantly.

"Oh, nothing much, just a little thing," I answer shyly, knowing that I am perhaps the only person ever to write such a description.

I wake up. Where are my glasses? What time is it? I reach out for clock and glasses, as if to convince myself that it really is June 21, 1981, not 1931.

At 4:45 the white garden gate opens and Henriette steps out—all ninety-seven years of her. She's wearing sensible brown shoes, wool stockings, a tan raincoat, and a loose-fitting wool tam. Her eyesight must be good—no glasses. She carries a cane, but she hardly uses it. In fact, she sets off at a brisk clip. At first her face looks huge to me. Like a spy, I take some photos of her. I don't even feel ashamed.

I get out of the car to follow her to the abbey, a little more than a block away. Inside the church, she sits down about halfway up the aisle, on the left, alone in a pew. I sit five or six rows behind her and on the right. About ten other people, mostly old, drift in singly and go up the aisle to sit near the front. The bells chime and Vespers begins.

The communion grille—a low fence—separates the congregation from the choir, from whose wings the monks, one at a time, cross back and forth, their hands folded beneath robes. Then a bunch of them, fifty maybe, enter from the left in triple file and arrange themselves in rows on the left, parallel to the nave. I can barely see the ones in the front row. The singing begins.

The sound is serious, calm, simple, utterly beautiful. It spreads evenly throughout the cool, dim air. The believers among us bow and cross themselves, and from time to time they stand up and sit down. I decide to relax and remain seated, though every once in a while I stand up. It occurs to me that the monks get a lot of rehearsal time but that the rehearsal is in some way also the performance. The audience is God.

Henriette, who, if she has attended this service five days a week since moving to Solesmes, has heard Vespers more than 16,000 times, anticipates everything by a beat. I alternate between watching her and looking at the gray blocks of stone, the stark, simple, romanesque arches along the sides and the Gothic vaulting over the nave. I wonder what the interior looked like in 1926, and in 1960. When Pierre sat here he must have been funneled down the narrow nave toward the altar and its inevitable crucifix.

After thirty minutes, Henriette puts down her Vespers book, and a moment later the singing stops—she has already retrieved her cane and turned to start back down the aisle.

I follow her out and down the street. Soon I overtake her, and as I walk past I sneak a glance. Her face is very old, though—and this is the odd part—not particularly wrinkled, and her dark little eyes remind me of those of a wily dog.

A bus is coming up the street, her street, toward her. She steps aside and stops, in that silent way the elderly have of protesting an affront. The bus goes past, and she resumes her walk. In the middle of the block (the safest place) she crosses diagonally, and when she gets to the opposite curb she spots something in the gutter, probably a leaf. She stops and swipes at it with her cane, two, three times, until she manages to move it to the right a few inches. That accomplished, she approaches the gate, inserts her key, and goes inside.

But the gate doesn't close. She reappears, holding a small, bright blue plastic bag tied at the top. She plops it down outside the gate, near the wall. The top part of the bag (above the tie) seems to bother her. She bats at it weakly with her hand, to force it to the side. She doesn't like the way it looks. She pushes at it again, then again. It's still not right. She picks up the bag and plops it down a few inches away from its original position. Then she pokes it. It sits there, sagging. She looks at it, pauses, and closes the gate. She's gone.

I start the car and drive back up to the corner. It's 5:45, the light is failing, and a chill is in the air. I wonder where I should spend the night. The only hotel in town, the Grand Hôtel, looks ritzy and expensive, compared to the other places I've been staying in. Nearby Sablé has cheaper hotels. In the midst of Reverdy's tomb, Henriette's vast old age, the monastery, the spirituality of the chant, and the onset of dark, I pause for a moment and head toward the Grand Hôtel.

In the room, I step out onto a balcony. Below is the hotel's pretty garden, and off to the left, a block away, still visible in the early evening, is the house Pierre Reverdy died in.

A Picture of Edwin

I hadn't felt ashamed, really deeply ashamed of myself, for a long time. I had frequently questioned my behavior and sometimes felt embarrassment, but not that burning, moral sinking that shame spreads throughout the viscera. Not being a Catholic who can be delivered of this feeling, in a confessional, I have to enter my own form of it, the voice box, and hope then to be done with it.

It goes like this.

As publishers of Edwin Denby's *Collected Poems,* Joan Simon and I felt that we ought to encourage journalists to write about Edwin on the occasion of his eightieth year. Joan prepared a little press kit, which we sent to various journalists.

Several newspapers and magazines took our suggestion. One of them, a big "uptown" magazine that recently had been revived from the 1930s, wanted to include a photograph of him. They would send a "car" to pick him up and take him home. It was up to me to get Edwin to consent to being photographed. I called him.

"Edwin, would you do me a favor?"

"Yes!"

"Would you let someone take your picture? It's for Full Court Press."

"Yes!"

"How about next week?"

"Yes!"

"I'll call you. Thanks."

"Okay!"

So it was all arranged. I intentionally did not tell him the name of the magazine or the photographer.

From *Blood Work* (Bamberger Books, 1993).

When I went to pick Edwin up, the limousine was waiting downstairs. The driver was perplexed: there was no buzzer, no nameplate, and the door was locked, in this somewhat down-at-the-heels loft building on anonymous Twenty-first Street.

"So what's this guy's claim to fame?" he asked good-naturedly.

"He's a great man. And he's the best writer on dance this world has ever seen. And he's a wonderful poet."

When I got upstairs, Edwin was confused. He thought the photographer was coming to shoot him at home, so he had made coffee and straightened the place up. But now he has to go out! Where are his glasses? The ones for distance. Where are his keys? His coat? Did I know about that new rainwear that is exactly like ordinary clothes but that sheds rain, you don't even need an umbrella? It's sold in only one shop somewhere uptown. Had I found out anything about that Bulgarian man who as a child had wandered with his family penniless but always attended the best schools in Italy and Spain and who had just won the Nobel Prize? Where are the keys? What about underwear? These are the wrong pants, they're not comfortable, have to change them. Are these the reading glasses? And then Edwin turned to me.

"I can't remember anything anymore, and I can't do two things at the same time. What is this picture for?"

"It's for Full Court Press."

"How exactly?"

"It's to be in a magazine and give publicity to your book."

"A magazine? Oh, I'll have to get my magazine face! If it's *Atlantic Monthly*, I'll look like this."

He made a face that was something like a cross between an austere scowl and a highfalutin grin.

"What magazine is it?" he went on.

"It's *Vanity Fair*."

His face took on a look of revulsion, and he pinched his nose. I started to smile. Then he looked me right in the eye and with utter seriousness said, one word at a time, "Those people stink, and I'm surprised you can't smell them too."

I stopped.

"Edwin, the magazine *does* stink and I *can* smell it."

"Then why are you doing this?"

"I think it will help the press. We're in debt and I'm trying everything to get us out."

"I doubt this will have any effect whatever."

"You're probably right, but I feel I have to try everything."

There was a pause, and I knew what to say.

"Look, Edwin, we don't have to do this. Really. I'll call them and say we can't make it."

"No, no, no, you said we'd be there, so let's be there."

"Are you sure?"

"Yes, of course. I'll survive."

I helped him downstairs and into the limousine. We both looked completely out of place in its immense, plush seats. My legs felt short.

A few minutes later, the limousine pulled up at the photographer's building. Waiting for us outside was a young woman from the magazine, a pretty and polite girl I liked right away. She seemed tactful.

Upstairs we were welcomed by the photographer. He was effusively cordial, even obsequious, almost trembling at the prospect of photographing Edwin. I didn't like his pear-shaped body. I didn't like his face. I didn't like his voice.

"Do you know *Vanity Fair?*" he asked Edwin.

"No," Edwin lied perfectly, "but I've heard of it. I knew the magazine in the '30s."

"Yes, of course," gushed the photographer. "We are trying to maintain the same high standards as the old *Vanity Fair,* and yet do something new and different, while bringing some *class* to it. There are so many terrible magazines these days, such as *People.* Do you know *People?*"

"No, I don't believe I do," Edwin replied pleasantly.

"Trash! Just trash about people one has never even heard of!" and seeing that Edwin had nothing to say to this, he raised his hand and said, "Well, shall we go into the studio?"

We were ushered into a room equipped with special lighting fixtures and something like a little stage setting: a bright white backdrop flanked by two black wings, and in the center a plain little table. In the darkness of the studio flitted four or five assistants who I think were mostly boys. They all looked identical.

Edwin was seated at the table, and the camera was brought

in close. The assistants held electrical instruments to his face and popped bright strobe lights. Pop. Pop. Pop. Then another kind of pop.

"That's good," oozed the photographer. "Now lift your head a little. Beautiful. Beautiful. Now bring your hand up, no, higher, there, now hold it, hold it, beautiful, just lovely."

Popflash.

"Now turn your head a little to the left and hold it, hold it, beautiful!"

Popflash.

"Look up, higher, tilt your head back, now think a beautiful thought, a perfectly *lovely* thought, hold it!"

Popflash.

"Now turn toward me, smile, let's see a big smile, bigger, bigger, your biggest smile! That's good, beautiful, now hold it and think a *beautiful* thought, hold that *beautiful* thought!"

Popflash.

And so it went, with the spook assistants tiptoeing about, moving light standards, popping bright strobes, and whispering in the wings, until finally Edwin let his face drop into his hands.

"Are you all right?" asked the photographer.

"Yes. . . . It's just that I've run out of beautiful thoughts."

I burst out laughing, relieved to be able to blow out some tension built up by watching Edwin restrain himself, hiding ever further and further from the camera, all the while displaying extraordinarily good manners. I couldn't stand it anymore. The session paused for a lens change.

I strode forward and said, "Edwin, is this okay? If you're tired we can stop." I put my hand over his.

"No, I'm fine."

He was not fine.

I wanted out of there.

The next series of shots went more quickly, and finally the photographer leaned back and announced, "Well, there! I think we've got a picture!"

Edwin and I edged toward the door, the genteel thank-you's and smiles of the photographer raining down on us. It was like being coated with slime, an expensive, thin slime.

When I saw the limousine downstairs, I told the girl we wouldn't need it, we would walk back. She thanked us and got into the limo.

"I insist on buying you a sandwich," I said to Edwin.

"Fine, and let's invite Billy MacKay, too, he works right up there at Barnes & Noble."

We took a few steps. I stopped and turned to Edwin.

"Edwin," I said, "I'm going to say this once, and I don't want to have to keep saying it: I'm sorry. I am very sorry. I'm ashamed of myself for getting you into this."

"No, no, don't be, it was very interesting, it was very interesting that this man hurts his subjects with those lights and can't possibly get a better result than Rudy, who wouldn't dream of causing his subjects any discomfort."

"And he's famous and Rudy isn't. Could there be any connection?"

Edwin laughed. "I wouldn't be surprised."

We stepped into Barnes & Noble and picked up Billy MacKay with his wild hair and beard that never left the '60s, and we went to a coffee shop and had coffee and English muffins and rice pudding. I was glad to have someone else there, to change the atmosphere, to put any kind of fresh experience between us and the picture session.

Outside again, Billy said goodbye and went back to work. It had started to mist. I took off my blue corduroy baseball cap and put it on Edwin's silver head. He looked beautiful.

"This'll keep the damp off your head."

"I don't really need it. You know, I like the rain. I like to walk in it. There are only two things that really excite me, walking in the rain and taking a cold shower. When you get old, you're not so sensitive to thrills anymore, but walking in the rain and taking a cold shower still thrill me."

We walked down to Fourteenth Street to find him some underwear, "smooth cotton longies," as he kept describing them to various Hispanic and Asian shopkeepers, but it was April and no store had long underwear in stock. I guess there aren't enough old people with poor circulation who are cold when everyone else is warm. Edwin appreciated my walking with him in search of long underwear. We walked back up to his street.

As we talked in front of his building, Katie rode up on her bike with groceries for his dinner.

"How did it go?" she asked.

Before Edwin could answer I said, "Horrible!"

"No, no, the interesting thing is that for about forty-five minutes afterward I couldn't see very well and my eyes hurt. . . ."

I suddenly remembered that Edwin had only recently recovered from a lens implant operation.

"Oh, Jesus Christ, Edwin, I completely forgot about that!"

"No, it's all right, because after forty-five minutes my eyes recovered, and I can see fine now. I've learned that my eyes are more resilient than I thought, and I wouldn't have found that out any other way."

"Where'd you get that hat, Edwin? It looks like Ron's," Katie said.

"Oh, yes, here." Edwin reached for the cap.

"No, it looks great on you. Keep it. I have another one at home anyway. And speaking of home, I've got to go." Then I said, "Edwin, thank you."

"You're welcome. And I still think you ought to write about that Bulgarian fellow."

On Edwin Denby

It is unusual for a poet's first collection from a major publisher to be a *Complete Poems*. In Edwin Denby's case, however, it is understandable. Edwin never "built his career" as poet. He never did anything to make his poetry known to a wide audience. In fact, by the 1960s he had become skittish about having his poetry published at all.

His first book, *In Public, In Private* (1948), had shown signs of this nervousness. The first edition, published by Decker Press in Prairie City, Illinois, was followed by a second edition only a few months later, not because the first had sold out but because Edwin (in New York and preparing to go to Europe) saw the need for alterations. He revised certain lines, dropped one poem, and corrected typographical errors. There must have been a certain amount of torment in seeing a whole new group of mistakes in the second edition. Edwin, his friends, and one of his brothers had underwritten the cost of both editions.

They also subsidized the second collection of poems, *Mediterranean Cities* (1956). This time, perhaps in reaction to the misprints in *In Public, In Private*, Edwin chose an outstanding printer, the Stamperia Valdonega in Verona, Italy. The production was handled by mail, with manuscripts, photographs, and proofs shuttling back and forth between Verona and New York. I suspect Edwin intentionally maintained his geological distance from the production of this book, as he had with *In Public, In Private*.

Despite their literary excellence, these books did not reach a large audience. Neither Decker Press nor George Wittenborn, Inc. (credited on the title page of *Mediterranean Cities* as

Originally appeared as the introduction to Edwin Denby's *Complete Poems* (Random House, 1986).

its publisher) had an advertising, sales, or distribution system for poetry. And Edwin's modesty, perhaps a result of his being well brought up, disallowed his behaving as though the public should admire him. His friends knew that an easy way to make him nervous was to praise him, especially for the wrong reasons: he would quickly change the subject or glance nervously toward the nearest exit. But people did admire him, a small, select audience of friends and those who were to become friends; poets such as Frank O'Hara and James Schuyler; painters such as Willem and Elaine de Kooning, Alex Katz, and Neil Welliver; composers such as Virgil Thomson and Aaron Copland; dancers and choreographers such as Merce Cunningham, Tanaquil LeClerc, and Paul Taylor; and his close friend Rudy Burckhardt, whose photographs were an added delight in Edwin's books.

In the early 1960s a new wave of admirers began to arrive. These young poets, painters, and dancers ferreted out rare copies of Edwin's books and, in their youthful ardor, tended to view him as a sort of living legend. Chief among them was Ted Berringan, the poet and editor. When Ted admired the work of someone who was, in his opinion, neglected, he set about correcting the situation. He wrote and spoke about Edwin's work with such conviction and persuasiveness that one was left with no choice but to read Edwin's poetry and begin to see for oneself.* Ted brought the same magnanimous intensity to the special Edwin Denby issue of his magazine *C* (1963), the first Denby collection of poems published by someone other than the author. I was with Ted the August night he swooped down on Edwin and declared that he was going to do the issue and that it would appear in a few weeks, so Edwin should now

---

*Ted "converted" me. I had first read Edwin's poetry in *Locus Solus,* no. 1 (1961), but I don't remember when I first met him in the following few years. My most vivid early memory of him is of running into him at a double feature of Hammer horror films at the New Yorker Theater in late 1963—he was doing "research" for his mad scientist role in Burckhardt's film *Lurk*—and his coming back to my apartment for coffee and conversation. He became only mildly discombobulated when I asked him to autograph my copy of *In Public, In Private.*

please immediately give him some new, unpublished poems to go with the older ones. Edwin, disarmed by this irrepressible Irishman, could hardly refuse what apparently was a fait accompli. The issue did in fact appear soon after, each copy bearing original silk-screened front and back covers by Andy Warhol, with an arresting image of Edwin being kissed by a young man. Edwin had little to say in all this.

This was equally true of his next collection, *Snoring in New York* (1974), copublished by Anne Waldman of Angel Hair and Larry Fagin of Adventures in Poetry. Comprised mostly of Edwin's later sonnets, this booklet served as an advance glimpse into another volume, already in preparation, his *Collected Poems*.

The *Collected Poems* was published in 1975 by Full Court Press (Anne Waldman, Joan Simon, and me). We knew we couldn't wait for Edwin's permission to print the book: he would hesitate forever. So we simply told him we were starting a publishing company and that the first book would consist of his poems. We didn't elicit the kind of conversation that would give him a chance to delay or refuse. Anytime he did mutter something about how no one would want to read his poetry because it was "just old stuff and not good enough," it was we who changed the subject and glanced toward the exit.

Right up to the publication of the *Collected Poems,* Edwin feared it would become overblown. He adamantly refused to allow the book to be called *The Complete Poems,* even though he had pretty much stopped writing poetry by then. That title sounded too pompous, too "uptown," for him (and perhaps too final). Also, he would not let us publish five of his later sonnets because he was "still working on them."

Without our knowing it, he paid someone else to correct his proofs. Was he unable to bear what he felt to be the inadequacies of his poetry, or did the poetry have such evocative power for him that it was too painful to reread? Or both?

The *Collected Poems* received highly favorable notices. Bill Zavatsky wrote: "Denby's *Collected Poems* is an important Baedecker by a sharp-eyed man who has noted down, with love, what most of us rush right past. Delightful work."[1] Jona-

---

1. *New York Times Book Review,* October 17, 1976.

than Galassi praised it as "a living, breathing, unusually valuable book by a poet who should be better known."[2] Hayden Carruth noted that Edwin had "been around for years actually, but fugitive, very fugitive" and that Edwin's work has "the enduring voice of poetry, the essential voice which carries on in spite of everything that fashion and literary politics can do to silence it."[3] Michael Lally echoed these sentiments: "It's obvious from [Denby's] work that many poets have been influenced by it, but where are the critics who mention it, or the anthologies that include it? This is not the incidental poetry of an eminent dance critic, or the work of an underground cult figure, but the work of a unique and major voice in contemporary poetry."[4] The consensus was one of bewilderment that this work had not been available before and of gratitude that now it was.

Edwin's reaction to all this was typically ambivalent. Rudy Burckhardt told me that Edwin claimed he didn't like all the attention but that deep down he was pleased by it. It was not the embittered pleasure of someone "recognized" too late or the preening pleasure of the vain. It was the pleasure of an old gentleman who had realized that his work was well loved.

The *Complete Poems* includes all the poems in the 1975 *Collected Poems,* some of which had appeared with typographical errors, others that Edwin revised slightly. (In December 1982 he gave me a list of such corrections and revisions, which stand as the final ones.) To these works I have added a few untitled poems that have never appeared in book form: " 'It takes all kinds,' the hackie's saw"; "In a hotelroom a madman"; "At first sight, not Pollock, Kline scared"; "The newspaper lies slid, tracked up"; "In tooth and claw red, not nature"; and two versions of "Old age, lookit, it's stupid, a big fart." Edwin would probably have objected to their inclusion. It was only after his death, in looking through his manuscripts and notebooks, that I realized how hard he had worked on his later poems, revising them over and over, scratching out lines and then restoring them, only to scratch them out again. He

---

2. *Poetry* (December 1976).
3. *Bookletter,* March 15, 1976.
4. *Washington Post Book World,* February 8, 1976.

worked several sonnets so hard that they slimmed down to only thirteen lines.

This *Complete Poems* does not include, of course, every poem Edwin wrote and saved. I have excluded poems written in adolescence, poems in a fragmentary state, and poems he had abandoned but not discarded. Not that there are many such pieces. In fact, given that he occupied the same loft for almost half a century, it is surprising how few papers he did keep. His austerity was pervasive. He was anything but his own archivist; he never dated his manuscripts, he never made marginal notes other than "out," "reject," or "keep," and he never kept his papers in any particular order. Finally, he made no special attempt to preserve them; as of this writing, the early manuscript versions of the poems in *In Public, In Private* and most of those in *Mediterranean Cities* remain lost.

Although Edwin was ambivalent about seeing his poetry in print and never played any standard role of "the poet," it is clear, from works such as the following undated, unrevised, and unpublished piece, that he did see himself as part of a literary tradition, a "print of voices" from Walt Whitman to himself to Frank O'Hara:

> Moved by a three A.M. breeze, an empty paper bag scrapes on the floor at the back of the loft—a thief sound—a wind from building to building bayward where the tide flows— exposed alone to electric light I sit reading poems of Frank O'Hara's—the print of voices dead Walt heard nervously in barroom and bedroom and I did and Frank does—the summer, the winter, a voice's fleshly furtive circling pitch among voices closeby, echoing Manhattan island closeby and far like Venice or Rotterdam or Leningrad or Foochow to be obliterated friends asleep on salt water sites or by electric light reading recent poems nearly single in the heat at night hearing the police or song behind a wall, a recent century of multiple acquainted voices, closeby, far off, silly, unobliterated, mine too, yours too.

Edwin Orr Denby was born on February 4, 1903, in Tientsin, China. His father, Charles Denby Jr., the American Consul in Tientsin and later a businessman, had met his mother, Martha Orr, in Peking, where her family had stopped on a trip around the world. Martha Orr's father was a businessman too, and both the Denby and the Orr families were from Evansville, Indiana. Edwin's grandfather, Charles Denby Sr., had served as minister to China in the mid-1880s, and he was illustrious enough to have the Charles Denby cigar named after him. Edwin was named after his paternal uncle, who was secretary of the navy under Harding and who had the honor of throwing out the first ball in Yankee Stadium. In 1924, however, charged with neglect of duty in the Teapot Dome scandal, he resigned, apparently a scapegoat.

After stays in Washington, D.C., and Hannover, Germany, the Denbys returned to China. One of Edwin's early memories was "at age four, that was in Shanghai . . . I remember the house, and pagoda, that marvelous thing with the great big tower in the back yard was overturned outside the wall of our garden, and it was so amazing to see it lying there on the ground."[5] The image of the pagoda—the exotic edifice that is both tower and temple, with curled-up eaves on its roofs that diminish as they gracefully rise—sideways on the ground can be applied in some respects to Edwin and his work. From birth—an American born in China—he was out of place. Dislocation, though, brought surprise and pleasure as well as the isolation of being different. His dislocation in China was doubled: he was not only removed from America, but, like his two older brothers and most of the other children of diplomats and foreign businessmen, he was restricted to the European community, removed from the Chinese.

Unlike the pagoda, however, Edwin was throughout his life mobile and fascinated by mobility, the mobility of travel, of dancers, of his cats, of strolling through the streets, and of thought.

When his family left Shanghai (in 1908, after Edwin's tonsils were removed) they settled in Vienna, where his father had another diplomatic appointment. Edwin received his early schooling in Vienna, where he learned German and saw his first ballet, *Die Puppenfee* (*The Fairy Doll*), which made a powerful impression on him. He was having dinner with his

---

5. In an interview with Mark Hillringhouse, *Mag City*, no. 14 (1983).

family on vacation at one of the grand hotels at the Lido when the outbreak of World War I was announced. Again Edwin was to find himself in an incongruous situation: eventually his family had to leave Austria, "the enemy country we had all liked so much."[6]

Returning for the first time to live for an extended period in the country of his nationality, he briefly attended private school in Detroit, where his father took a position as vice president of the Hupp Motor Company. In 1916 Edwin was sent to Hotchkiss, the Connecticut preparatory school. He had started writing poetry around the age of twelve and by fourteen showed a precocious talent for the sonnet, as shown in his second published poem:

Sonnet

Then, in the dewy even-tide of years,
We'll sit together, while the feline night
Steals silently without, and the faint light
Of low-burned candles trembles as wind nears;
We'll sit together on the rude-carved bench
I made for you when first our eyes had met.—
Ah! What a moment—Ne'er shall I forget
Those eyes,—whose light of trust no years can quench.
Then will the fiery passions of the May
Of Life be tempered by maturer age;
Then eyes will dim and thin the golden tress,
And cheeks grow pale—past long their triumph day.
And though not far the threatening death-storms rage,
Yet Love lives in the bare boughs none the less![7]

At Hotchkiss he wrote sonnets influenced by Milton, Wordsworth, and Shelley. He also wrote the class poem. In his senior year he was voted "The Biggest Grind" by his classmates, "those other fellows whom I didn't get along with."[8] Edwin had an outstanding scholastic record; his scores on the college entrance examinations were the highest in the country. In

---

6. Quoted in John Gruen, *The Party's Over Now* (New York: Viking, 1972), 162.

7. *Hotchkiss Literary Monthly* (May 1917).

8. Hillringhouse interview.

1919 he graduated, winning the Phi Beta Kappa trophy and the Greek and English prizes. Hotchkiss was a feeder school for Yale; Edwin, not yet seventeen, went to Harvard.

His freshman year was academically outstanding, but in December 1920, in the middle of his sophomore year, he abruptly left school and took a steamer to England with classmate Frank Safford. They expected to go there and make their fortunes, but they soon returned, penniless, and this slender, sensitive, well-traveled young poet took a job for five months on a New Hampshire farm.

Seeing no other option, he went back to Harvard in 1921 for another year but was not happy there, cutting classes, reading poetry, drinking, dreaming, and talking with a few good friends, feeling "wanderlust," and hoping to write someday "with fire."[9]

Edwin did not return to Harvard for his junior year. Instead, he and Safford quit school again and moved (with Safford's wife) to New York City "to study and write," neither of which they did. Typically, Edwin landed an unsuitable job (with the New York Telephone Company), which he quit after five months because, although he understood perfectly well the abstract wiring diagrams, he was bewildered by masses of real wires. His parents must have been apprehensive about him, but they gave him some money, and with it he went in 1923 to Vienna, partly because Safford was going to study medicine there.

To keep his parents happy, Edwin enrolled in a few courses at the University of Vienna. On the train, returning to Vienna after a vacation, he fell into conversation with a young woman who invited him to see the Hellerau-Laxenburg School, where she was studying dance. Urged on by friends, and to keep his promise to her, he visited the school. Soon afterward he enrolled and took his first dance lessons. Again, he found himself out of place: he was one of the few male students.

There were, however, more fundamental problems than this. He had doubtless dismayed his parents by dropping out of college and not getting ahead. He seemed to have no marketable skills, no place in society. And by now he, who had

---

9. From an unpublished diary.

been dismayed by the snickering remarks of homophobic college classmates, must have recognized that he was having trouble coming to terms with his sexuality. During this period in Vienna he experienced depression and considered suicide but "never had the nerve."[10] One day he knocked on Dr. Freud's door and was told that the doctor was indisposed but that Dr. Paul Federn, a colleague, could be consulted. Edwin underwent analysis with Dr. Federn for several years and later met Freud through him. Federn's other patients included (though not at the same time) Rilke, Wilhelm Reich, and Hermann Broch.

After three years (1925–28) at the Hellerau-Laxenburg School, Edwin received a diploma in gymnastics, which led to his specializing in *Grotesktanz* (eccentric dancing), a form of modern dance. After a brief period as a member of the dancing chorus of the State Theater of Darmstadt, he and his partner Claire Eckstein formed a small dance company. The group toured Germany (1928–33), appearing at the Berlin Wintergarten and receiving favorable reviews in German dance magazines that singled out his work for praise. Photographs of Edwin performing *Grotesktanz* reflect the image of the pagoda on its side: he is usually shown in surprising positions.

Two of his poems appeared in *Poetry* in 1926, apparently the first publication of his poetry in a national literary magazine. How this occurred remains unknown.

In 1927 his oldest brother, Charles, sent him round-trip fare so he could return to America for both brothers' weddings (which turned out to be prestigious affairs, with prominent guests attending James's wedding in Philadelphia and a week later President and Mrs. Coolidge attending Charles's in Washington, D.C.). Knowing that Edwin would have little interest in these social events, Charles assured him that he could spend the travel money any way he liked. So Edwin, the odd man out in his family, took a trip to Russia, staying for six weeks in Moscow. There, on a pass personally issued by Anatoly Lunacharsky—the writer, revolutionary, and powerful commissar of education in charge of theaters—he saw many productions (including one of Meyerhold's) and the Bolshoi Ballet.

---

10. Hillringhouse interview.

In 1929, with his passport still listing his occupation as "student," he returned to the State Theater of Darmstadt and spent a year as dancer, choreographer, and libretto adapter. His colleagues there included Wilhelm Reinking and Rudolf Bing. Edwin's German libretto *Die Neue Galathea,* an adaptation of Franz von Suppe's operetta *Die Schoene Galathea,* was performed in 1929 and published by B. Schott's Sons, Mainz. He tried, without success, to convince his colleagues to produce Gertrude Stein and Virgil Thomson's *Four Saints in Three Acts,* still unperformed at that time. In the late 1920s in Germany, Edwin met Aaron Copland, Bertolt Brecht, Kurt Weill, and Lotte Lenya. Much of Edwin's own output during this period—adaptations, stories, essays, perhaps poems and theater pieces—was written in German.

In Collioure, France, in 1930, Edwin met Virgil Thomson, who was to remain a lifelong friend. Considering Edwin's circle of acquaintances and his numerous if brief trips to Paris, it is odd that he never met Gertrude Stein, whose work had a noticeable influence on his poetry.

Germany grew increasingly dangerous, and because Edwin's satirical dances were considered politically suspect, he left in 1933. In Paris later that same year a performance of Balanchine's work—which he had first seen in 1930—struck him as "the most wonderful thing I had seen in my life," especially *Mozartiana.*[11] It was at this point that Edwin began to take a serious interest in ballet. In the 1940s he championed Balanchine in New York, and his admiration never wavered.

Edwin joined his family in Majorca, where he wrote the first draft of his only novel, *Scream in a Cave* (also called *Mrs. W's Last Sandwich*).

In 1934, in need of a new passport photo, he met the photographer-medical student Rudy Burckhardt in Basel. Having spent the past several years moving around Europe, Edwin returned to New York in 1935, soon followed by Burckhardt, and together they rented the cold-water, heatless, fifth-floor walk-up loft at 145 West 21 Street that he was to occupy

---

11. Interview with John Howell, *Performance Arts Journal #11* 4, nos. 1–2 (n.d.).

for the rest of his life. Though heat and hot water were later added, the loft always retained its austerity.

He soon became friends with his neighbor Willem (and soon thereafter Elaine) de Kooning. It was fortuitous and wonderful that they happened to live in the building just next door. Edwin and Burckhardt sat for de Kooning and were among the first to buy his work; that is, from time to time they gave him money when he needed it and from time to time he gave them a picture.

For the next ten years Edwin produced a great deal, mostly in New York, a city flooded with refugee artists and intellectuals. He wrote the poems published in 1948 as *In Public, In Private*. He also wrote adaptations and librettos: *Horse Eats Hat* with Orson Welles, a W.P.A. adaptation of Labiche and Michel's *Le Chapeau de paille d'Italie,* with incidental music by Paul Bowles orchestrated by Virgil Thomson (premiere in 1936, with Edwin playing the rear legs of the horse, designed by puppeteer Bil Baird); *The Second Hurricane,* an opera libretto with music by Aaron Copland (premiere in 1937); *The Sonntag Gang,* an opera libretto (completed in 1940); a ballet libretto, *The Death and Some Notes on the Life of Joe Bascom* (completed in 1941); and *Miltie Is a Hackie,* an opera libretto (completed in 1942). With Rita Matthias he translated Bruckner's play *The Criminals* (premiere in 1941). He also did the choreography (for the Boston premiere only) of the Maxwell Anderson–Kurt Weill musical *Knickerbocker Holiday* (1938) and appeared for the first of many times in films of Burckhardt's.

His librettos and adaptations are mostly about America, with high school students, cowboys, blacks, a jockey, a cab driver, and so on, using language that is often downright "down home." It is as though he were studying the same faces as those in the photographs of his friend Walker Evans. Edwin's "common man" subject matter, however, never quite took on the proletariat slant typical of the 1930s, for although he was antifascist (and even anticapitalist), he played no active part in politics. In writing about ordinary Americans, he was trying to see what it felt like to be one. He was also clarifying his language, making it simpler and sleeker. Like Gertrude Stein and William Carlos Williams, two other somewhat dislocated Americans, he worked with a simple vocabulary to express complex feelings. It should be added that Edwin took great pleasure in being in New York, among people he didn't particularly understand.

At Aaron Copland's suggestion he wrote articles on the dance (his first was "Noces," 1936) and that same year—again through Copland—began a regular dance review column ("With the Dancers") for Minna Lederman's *Modern Music,* partly, he claimed, as a way of getting free tickets. He credited Lederman with having taught him how to rein in his tendency toward poetic digression and to express himself more clearly in essay form.

In 1937 he passed through Puerto Rico and the Dominican Republic on his way to Haiti with Burckhardt, then went to stay in Mexico with Copland to work on *The Second Hurricane.*

After the bombing of Pearl Harbor, he tried to enlist in the army but was refused, apparently because of his age (nearly thirty-nine). At Virgil Thomson's invitation he worked as guest dance critic for the *New York Herald Tribune* from 1942 until 1945 (when the regular critic, Walter Terry, returned from war). Edwin's working pattern as a critic underwent a sudden change: the same critic who had labored painfully over every word in his *Modern Music* pieces could now finish a review for the morning edition a few hours after leaving an evening performance. The drain on his energy was telling, though, and he relinquished the job with as much relief as regret.

The appearance of his first book of poems, *In Public, In Private,* was delayed by the war until 1948. The scant critical response ranged from lukewarm to mixed to thoroughly negative. The most favorable notice, by Hubert Creekmore, praised Edwin's "flair for finishing off his poems with a meaningful couplet, for combining the traditional epigram with the lyric, and for ironic effects," for the "many truly astonishing images," and for their forming "a witty or revealing series of comments," but noted that the work needed more "focus and unification and smoothness," that it was "diffused in impact because subjectively organized."[12] British critic Nicolas Moore felt that, al-

---

12. *New York Times Book Review,* August 15, 1948.

though the poems' language and imagery were "striking," "Mr. Denby lacks control."[13] The two other American reviews were both by Dudley Fitts. In the *Kenyon Review*[14] he allowed that four of the poems were worthy of book publication, but in the *Partisan Review* he blasted the author for having "neither taste, nor ear, nor control," with little in the book other than "mishandled metres, a yammering diction, and a brash inconsequence of intent."[15] Given the prevailing poetic climate in the late 1940s, it is not hard to see how these reviewers mistook the compressed, quirky, big-city stop-and-go rhythms for lack of control. These rhythms have little to do with, say, the artful "sprung" rhythm of Gerard Manley Hopkins's poetry or even the fragmented measures of Pound's *Cantos*. The work in *In Public, In Private* is further complicated by its coupling of idiomatic language and traditional form, making Edwin a kind of unpredictable Shakespeare-Wordsworth of the streets. It was hard to categorize—and thereby understand—his poetry.

If these are hard poems to read, they are not hard in the usual ways: they are not recondite, they are not high-toned, they do not make literary allusions, they do not use "poetic" language. They are not even aggressively modernist or "experimental" (although in their own subtle way they are quite radical). Their difficulties lie elsewhere, particularly in their shifting tones.

Take, for instance, the first four lines of the first poem, "The Climate":

> I myself like the climate of New York
> I see it in the air up between the street
> You use a worn-down cafeteria fork
> But the climate you don't use stays fresh and neat

The first line seems like a simple enough beginning. But what's this word *myself* doing there? Its presence suggests that the first line is not the start of a train of thought but, rather, the continuation of an anterior clause such as "Some people

---

13. *Poetry Quarterly* (London) 10, no. 3 (Autumn 1948).
14. Vol. 11, no. 1 (Winter 1949).
15. Vol. 16, no. 4 (April 1949).

don't care for the weather here, but. . . ." The first line, then, has a little accent or inflection in the reflexive pronoun that shifts the tone of what would otherwise be an ordinary opening. The first line ends with no punctuation other than blank space, which in Edwin's poetry usually indicates a pause; he doesn't use punctuation marks unless they're necessary for clarity or emphasis.

Like the first line, the second uses simple language with a shift in it, but this time the shift is semantic. Oddly, the speaker *sees the climate,* which suggests a wider range of perception than does, say, seeing a cloud. What is more arresting, though, is that he uses the phrase "up between the street." *Street,* in this context, assumes its more inclusive meaning of pavement, curbs, sidewalks, and buildings. What is understood here is "up between the *sides* of the street," because obviously nothing can be between one thing.

Line 3 contains another tonal shift. What appears on first reading to be a flat statement is in fact inflected: there is emphasis on *use* (in the sense of "use up"): "You *use* a worndown cafeteria fork," in opposition to line 4, "But the climate you don't use stays fresh and neat." The unexpectedly domestic vocabulary ("fresh and neat") to describe something as intangible and all-encompassing as climate is another example of the delicate but significant moves in the poem.

These nimble shifts—a form of wit characteristic of Edwin's poetry—reinforce the theme of mutability: how we change and get used up but air changes and the climate (larger nature) stays the same. Even ecologists, I think, would not wish to argue with the poem's basic theme.

Another surprising move is taking place in this and in most of Edwin's poems: they are sonnets, modernized, yes, but Shakespearean sonnets nonetheless. In taking this tack, Edwin was going against the current of just about everything that was considered "advanced" at the time. (In a later, unpublished sonnet he wrote: "Aren't you ashamed to write sonnets / Of course, what are *you* ashamed of.")

In Public, In Private contains other shifts as well, from poem to poem: from rage and loathing ("A Sonnet Sequence") to spookiness ("Irish American Song"), from disgust for mankind ("The Poison") to humor ("Aaron" and "The Subway"), from contentment ("First Warm Days") to displacement ("In Salzburg"), from social alienation ("Elegy—The Streets") to warmth, friendship, and love ("A Postcard"). From the variousness of this book emerges the figure of a solitary, meditative man struggling to keep himself together and to see if he fits into the scheme of things—assuming there is one—and if we do.

These are poems to live with, to read over a period of time. The reader should expect them at first to be elusive, eccentric, or awkward, with a high density of thought. By reflecting alternately on their tones and meanings, however, one gradually acquires a sense of their wholeness and the particular craft behind that wholeness.

In 1948, Edwin returned to Europe for two years on a Guggenheim Fellowship to write a book about contemporary European dance. (Although he never wrote the book, he did write essays.) He went via North Africa, visiting Paul Bowles for three months in Tangiers. After his longest stay heretofore in America—thirteen years—Edwin seems to have wanted a taste of a distinctly different culture. He probably needed the reassurance and refreshment of feeling out of place again, free of the heady but aggressive and competitive New York atmosphere. He was also curious about Moroccan life, "fascinated by the relationships between people,"[16] as he was fascinated by the relations between dancer and dance, sky and street, self and nonself. He was introduced to hashish by Bowles but took too much and found himself, according to Burckhardt, wandering down some timeless hallway in his mind. Although Edwin had also once smoked opium with Cocteau in Paris, he never "used drugs" and was, after a brief romance with alcohol in college, a moderate drinker.

In 1949 his first volume of critical writing, *Looking at the Dance,* was published. Its pieces had been collected and edited by B. H. Haggin, with Edwin typically having little to do with it. Not only was *Looking at the Dance* one of the first, if not *the* first, collections of dance essays and reviews, it is still widely considered the best book ever written on the dance. Edwin, in Europe, was not present to enjoy the book's success.

His Guggenheim was extended for another two years after

---

16. Gruen, *Party's Over Now,* 165.

he fell ill and underwent an operation for a stomach ulcer. For some months after the operation he thought he was going crazy, only to learn later that mental disturbance was one of the possible side effects of the anesthetic.

During the period of his Guggenheim he traveled around Europe, and in 1951 he lived in Ischia for six months with the Burckhardts (Rudy, his wife Edith, and son Jacob). Together they toured Italy, Sicily, and Greece. It was in Ischia that Edwin met James Schuyler.

After returning to New York he met other poets and painters of the New York School: Larry Rivers, Jane Freilicher, Fairfield Porter, John Ashbery, Kenneth Koch, and Frank O'Hara. He was particularly close to O'Hara.

In 1955 he and Burckhardt went to Morocco and Italy for brief visits, which gave him the chance to put the finishing touches to the *Mediterranean Cities* manuscript. This book, in all likelihood written after 1948, was published with Burckhardt's photographs in 1956. Apparently it received only one review, by Frank O'Hara in *Poetry* magazine in 1957. In *Mediterranean Cities* the poet comes through not so much in what he says about himself as in what he says about things outside himself. From time to time there intrude suggestions of "uneasiness," "the crunch of anguish," "our unlimited dark," and "tearing grief," but there is no evidence that it is the poet who is feeling them; besides, the expression of such personal feelings is not the main thrust of these sonnets, in which the poet's sensibility is turned outward toward the contemporary settings of what was in ancient times called Greater Greece.

This turning outward may have been an outgrowth of Edwin's work as a dance critic, which required that he focus his attention externally, see clearly without prejudice, and then write about what he saw. Not surprisingly, the infrequency of the "I" in these poems did not squelch the poet's presence but made it more pervasive, as his sensibility is discovered not in the largeness of the self but in the largeness of the world.

There is immediate pleasure in the lushness of language in *Mediterranean Cities* but also a complexity of syntax and meaning that comes clear only with sustained attention. In "Venice," for example, the first four lines are euphonious and haunting:

> She opens with the gondola's floated gloze
> Lapping along the marble, the stir of swill
> Open to night sky like in tenement hallways
> The footfalls, and middream a bargeman's lone call;

but the relationship of the clauses and phrases isn't obvious. What is doing the lapping? What is open to the night sky— "she," the swill, or the footfalls? The mysteriousness of relationships is even deeper in what might be called the second stanza (ll. 5–8), which is almost cubistic in its displacements:

> Sideways leading to her green, her black, like copper
> Like eyes, on tide-lifted sewers and façades
> Festooning people, barges a-sway for supper
> Under hunched bridges, above enclosed pink walls.

The sense is clarified when one realizes that *green* probably refers to verdigris, but even then the piling up of planes is dizzying.

Next comes an abrupt shift from cityscape to individual:

> And crumbling sinks like a blond savory arm
> Fleshed, a curled swimmer's pale belly that presses
> And loosens, and moist calves, then while the charm
> Subsides, Venice secrets pleases, caresses.

It is almost as if the city, the "she," had been making love, or had by osmosis become the swimmer making love to her, for the gender of the swimmer is not disclosed, any more than the particular kind of lovemaking going on. Something erotic happens. The experience subsides, and we are returned to

> The water-like walking of women, of men
> The hoarse low voices echo from water again

where the poem began.

Venice's two extremes—its picturesque gondolas and its unattractive swill—are subsumed into its liquid, dreamy, sensuous, mysterious, ambiguously erotic nature, and we are left floating gently in its wake. The language does not merely provide an attractive description of a foreign place, it embodies the union of sensibility and place. This particular Venice cannot be experienced unless the reader becomes, for a moment, the poet, who has, for a moment, become Venice.

Just as the other places in *Mediterranean Cities* are not so mazelike and hermetic as Venice, the other poems in it are not so difficult. There are lighter moments, even some expressions of outright happiness, rare in so meditative a poet. (This is not to imply that meditation necessarily brings unhappiness.) The work is milder, less violent, more classical than that in *In Public, In Private*. The poems are permeated with history, but history taken personally, which enables the poet to give a richer sense of the way things are in any particular place. These poems are more public than private; or, rather, the private is discovered in the public.

Edwin occasionally ventured beyond the sonnet form. "Elegy—The Streets" in *In Public, In Private* has its mate in the later "Snoring in New York—An Elegy." The latter was written over a long period, but exact dating is difficult, other than to note that the poem first appeared in *Locus Solus* magazine in 1962. On the whole it is more developed in theme and sophisticated in technique than its earlier counterpart, in which the pain of disappointed love drives the poet out into the street, where he seeks the consolation of society. In "Elegy" his rage is "but a dream." In "Snoring," on the other hand, his dreams are invaded by the sounds and appearances of people in the street, as he submits to "the advances of madness" along the borderline where sleeping and waking, anguish and gladness, are interchangeable. The poem's language slides back and forth, too, between straightforward declaration and baffling ellipsis, with an undertow of sexuality.

This poem was published in revised form in 1974 with Edwin's last collection of sonnets, written most likely in the late 1950s and early 1960s. In these later sonnets (which Edwin never named) the rhyme has become looser, stanza breaks done away with, formality of tone left behind. The pace is quicker, the tone more personal, the mind more nimble. The sureness of gesture is comparable to the drawings of a master artist whose training and technique have become a part of his physiology, so that if his heart is true, then his line can never be wrong.

Edwin's later sonnets exemplify a wonderful balance between poet in the world and world in the poet. They are the poems of a man entering ripe maturity, with the richness of a whole life's experience, a poet writing for himself, with nothing to gain or lose by it, a poet for whom no idea is too large, no moment too small. For sheer attentiveness these poems are unsurpassed. The themes are those of solitude, loneliness, joy, astonishment, change, curiosity about others, kindness, anger, despair, death, the miracle of consciousness, and sympathy for the things of this world. The elemental power of places (New York City, rural Maine, Europe, the ocean) infuses daily life with a majesty and fascination that are also quite natural. Although in one poem Edwin describes himself as out of place, "an interloper," what resonates in these poems is an acceptance of this role.

In 1963 the special Edwin Denby issue of Ted Berrigan's *C* magazine appeared. Between 1963 and 1983 these other publications followed, none of them initiated by Edwin: *Dancers, Buildings and People in the Streets,* a second volume of essays, in 1965; *Mrs. W's Last Sandwich,* originally *Scream in a Cave* (1972); *Miltie Is a Hackie* (1973); *Snoring in New York* (1974); *Collected Poems* (1975); *The Sonntag Gang* (1983, in a special Denby issue of *Mag City* magazine). Some of these went through several printings and editions.

Edwin's sixty-ninth birthday was celebrated by a reading of his poems at the St. Mark's Poetry Project in 1972. To everyone's surprise, Edwin not only attended, he even read one of his poems ("Elegy—The Streets"), something he had always declined to do publicly. His reading manner was natural and conversational, his tone serious but agile. His reading made it remarkably easy to follow the contours of the poetry.

Dance magazine had given him its award in 1965. He attended the ceremony and even gave an acceptance speech, albeit one that trailed off. In 1979, he received the Brandeis University Notable Achievement Award. For the latter his friends had to drag him to the presentation at the Guggenheim Museum. Never before had the pagoda image been more obvious; Edwin, who was receiving the most prestigious award, sat on stage looking like an uncomfortable but luminous schoolboy as the other recipients made gracious acceptance speeches.

When his turn came—the climax of the proceedings—he stunned everyone by striding stiffly to the podium and saying "thank you" and darting straight back to his chair.

His *Four Plays,* short dialogue pieces written for an Andy Warhol film that was never made, was produced in 1981 by the Eye and Ear Theatre in New York. Surprisingly, he attended many rehearsals and performances, taking great interest and delight in the production.

Although Edwin wrote little poetry or criticism in the last twenty years of his life—he kept revising his new pieces out of existence—his cultural life flourished. He could usually be found at performances of the New York City Ballet, Merce Cunningham, or Paul Taylor, and he closely followed the work of young choreographers of modern dance, as well as the many ethnic dance companies that performed in New York. He also frequently attended poetry readings by young poets. In the late 1960s he took an active interest in Robert Wilson's theatrical company, the Byrd Hoffman School of Byrds, and he never missed a show by painters he admired.

Edwin was very sociable. He enjoyed the company of his friends, with whom he dined virtually every night. He had a hearty appetite and a taste for good food. His conversation was brilliant, calm, and sometimes breathtakingly digressive (often causing some of his friends to regret that they didn't have a concealed tape recorder handy when they ran into him). As Frank O'Hara had written about him, "He sees and hears more clearly than anyone else I have ever known."

After 1965 he spent part of each summer in Searsmont, Maine, with Burckhardt and Yvonne Jacquette, the painter, at the rural house they all owned together. Across the road from the house are fields, a pine woods, and the big pond mentioned in Edwin's later sonnets. Not far away were other friends, such as Alex and Ada Katz and Neil Welliver. To Edwin's frustration, he couldn't complete a long essay on Burckhardt's work, which he had liked so much for so long.

A confirmed night person, he frequently went for walks alone around his (not particularly safe) New York City neighborhood, sometimes quite late at night, returning home alone to his cats. His slender build, silver hair, white skin, and blue eyes, his graceful manner, his attractive modesty, his inwardness, surprising in so public a man—all went toward giving him a kind of radiance or spirituality. The book he read most in his last years was *The Divine Comedy* (*Purgatorio* and *Paradiso*—not *Inferno*) in Italian.

He bore the physical infirmities of old age with patience and even good humor, but what he could not bear was the disintegration of his mind, the onset of senility. On July 12, 1983, shortly after arriving in Maine, he sat down at a table, took an overdose of sleeping pills and alcohol, and left the world.

On Ted Berrigan's *Sonnets*

For years now, since the early 1960s at least, Ted Berrigan has kept a journal, where he probably made notes about the writing of *The Sonnets*. My memory of those details is hazy. Apparently the first sonnets were written in the winter and spring of 1963.

Ted was twenty-nine. The previous several years had seen him take up amphetamine; move to New York; become involved with several young women; write his master's thesis on George Bernard Shaw; return his M.A. certificate with the note, "Keep this, I am the master of no art"; live on the down and out, mostly by writing papers for students at Columbia, by bumming money from his friends, and by stealing, reading, and reselling the books he could not buy—an incredible number of those; striding at top speed from one movie theater, art gallery, and museum to another; drinking gallons of coffee and yakking all night and into the next day; hopping in a car, driving to New Orleans, marrying a girl he'd just met, spiriting her away from the Florida mental institution where her horrified parents had her incarcerated for such an impulsive marriage to such a dubious character, and going on the lam with her to Denver; and finally returning to the City, to a rented room on 113th Street between Broadway and Amsterdam.

In this room, with his young wife, his books, his records, his manuscripts, and his pills, he began the sonnets, the first four or five in one night, as I recall; then a chunk of three or four more, then more; and Ted, I believe, had to told his breath: *he*

An introduction to Ted Berrigan's reading of his *Sonnets* in its entirety in 1978. The talk was published in *Brilliant Corners* magazine, edited by Art Lange, and in *Nice to See You: Homage to Ted Berrigan* (Coffee House Press, 1991), edited by Anne Waldman.

was on to something. It was like a dream in which you find a suitcase that is filled with money, each bill a hundred, no! a thousand dollars. You can't believe your luck and the feeling sweeping over you! Ted seems to have sustained that magic moment throughout the writing of *The Sonnets,* which took only a few months.

In a sense, some of *The Sonnets* had already been written. Many of the lines he used were from previous poems of his or from translations or mistranslations he'd done. Some were entire poems he had written as far back as the fall of 1961— "Personal Poem #2" became "Sonnet LXXVI." Some lines were "lifted" out of poems by John Ashbery, Kenneth Koch, and Frank O'Hara or from Ted's immediate friends, such as Dick Gallup, Joe Brainard, and me. It was of course not a question of plagiarization—a term that sent us into spasms of laughter—it was a matter of using "found" lines to create an entirely different work, and the intention was, if I may use such a word here, honorable.

Ted had a license to operate in this no-holds-barred manner, a license granted by Duchamp, Tzara, Arp, and Ernst (and later Burroughs); particularly Duchamp, who was like a god to us. The heroic example of Abstract Expressionism (especially de Kooning, Pollock, and Hans Hofmann) was constantly before us, with each day big and exciting and "all-over." And—to help tie it all together—hadn't Frank O'Hara written a book on Pollock?

Anyway, at that time we didn't speak English, we spoke Poetry. Our conversation was studded with quotations from the poetry we idolized. If a supermarket were closing, we'd point and laugh and say, "The academy of the hamburger is closing its doors" (a variation on a John Ashbery line), or we'd say hello with something such as "I see you are wearing your pink Francis Picabia diapers today!" (a travesty of Kenneth Koch). Such pseudo-quotations ran from these contemporaries back to Stevens, Pound, Williams, Rimbaud, Conrad Aiken, and others (Shakespeare, Homer, Virgil, and Dante). Ray Charles, Miguel Aceves Mejia, Leadbelly, Woody Guthrie, Cisco Houston, Big Bill Broonzy, Eric Darling, our Caedmon records of modern poetry—especially Stevens's "Idea of Order at Key West," with its sibilance and stateliness and mysterious "sacred portals dimly starred"—and our Oscar Williams anthologies, these were all literally worn out in a period of several years, as Kerouac's and Ginsberg's books had been a few years before. We had become living anthologies of literature, striding, excited and harmlessly obnoxious, through the streets of New York rejoicing!

This does not explain, though, why *The Sonnets* was written—or rather built—when it was. My guess is that you can expand only so far without being blown to pieces and that it was time for Ted to consolidate. It is easy to point out the variousness of tones and influences in this work, less easy to describe the craftsmanship involved. I said "built" rather than "written" because, as Ted himself has said several hundred times, he was using words as though they were bricks he placed side by side, one course after another, tapping them into place with his old typewriter that required a firm wham of the fingers. Scissors and Elmer's glue were also essential tools.

Not a single poem in *The Sonnets* conforms to the classical definition of the sonnet, either Shakespearean or Italian, and yet the sense of the sonnet, the feel of the well-crafted "little song," hovers behind them all. Ted had written imitations of Shakespeare's sonnets a couple of years before. The changes he rung on the traditional sonnet form, with a good dose of the hypnotic repetition of lines in the pantoum form, are particularly interesting. The line enjambments, the twisting of syntax, the "push-pull" of meaning, the abrupt changes of tone, the dislocation of punctuation, the fading in and out of prosody, the intentional misuse of parts of speech, the aesthetic decisions as to when to accept the results of a chance operation or to discard them—these should not be overlooked in favor of colorful subject matter.

For personal reasons I wasn't seeing very much of Ted while he was writing *The Sonnets*, though we lived nearby and had the same friends. But by late spring of 1963, when he started *C* magazine, I was feeling friendlier, and by the spring of 1964 he had started publishing C Books. He edited my first collection and I edited the first edition of *The Sonnets*, four hundred copies with a beautiful cover by Joe Brainard, to whom the book is dedicated. Actually there was very little editing as such on either side. He produced what I wanted in my book, and I produced what he wanted in his. I remember typing the mimeograph stencils and marveling at the poems and at how I was seeing them in a way you can't see them unless you actually sit down and type them, almost as though you were writing them yourself.

A few years later Donald Allen at Grove Press published a new edition of *The Sonnets,* which went through two printings (6,000 copies) and is now out of print. Temporarily, I am sure.* Because, unlike so many poems Ted and I wrote in the early 1960s, and despite moments of sentimentality and self-importance, *The Sonnets* have held up, because the art is good. They *are* feminine, they *are* marvelous, they *are* tough.

---

*The Sonnets was reprinted by United Artists in 1982 and by Penguin in 2000. (Ed.)

Three Book Reviews

The three book reviews gathered here came from my admiration for their subjects and from my impatience with conventional book reviews. All three pieces appeared in Kulchur *magazine, edited by Lita Hornick. The review of Edward Gorey (in* Kulchur *16 [Winter 1964–65]) shows a debt to Andy Warhol in its repetitions and to Joe Brainard in its use of the rubber stamp. In fact, Joe gave me the kit the rhinoceros stamp came from. My youthful subversiveness took an extreme turn (in* Kulchur *18 [Summer 1965]) when I reviewed a book that didn't exist, Joseph Ceravolo's* Wild Flowers Out of Gas *(which subsequently was published, by Tibor de Nagy Editions). The review of Ted Berrigan's* Sonnets *(Kulchur 17 [Spring 1965]) is composed entirely of lines and phrases from that book, an appropriative method that Ted himself used.*

Wild Flowers Out of Gas: Joseph Ceravolo: unpublished manuscript

Joe Ceravolo's poems are like the old lady who helps a Boy Scout across the busy street. They are also like the truck driver who stops his truck to let them cross safely, toots his horn, and waves. They are also like the nickel in the Boy Scout's pocket that was not bent by being run over by the truck.

The Sonnets: Ted Berrigan: C Press: $1

My dream is to have a drink with the people who wrote these poems. They mean "something." They mean to me what night letters from everyone I have ever known would mean to me. Perhaps I weep too much. Still, if you want your life to change, change your shirt the same way you must read from line to line, sonnet to sonnet, and line to sonnet, because many people, when reading these poems, all roar.

The romance of these poems is overwhelming, and of course it rains often in them outside the author's room in his head. In these sonnets the world in its mysteries is explained and at last extinct!

Santa Claus wrote this book as a technical journal and then walked out and looked for you. You made it hard to write. That's probably why there's this excitement to be all of night, and seeming wide night. Perhaps this is our one chance to have a big drink of waterbugs. Fortunately, Guillaume Apollinaire is dead.

Either these poems are feminine marvelous and tough or I am feminine marvelous and tough when I read them on the site of Benedict Arnold's triumph, Ticonderoga. It hurts. Au revoir, scene! I am forced to write "au revoir" when I mean "my hands make love to my body when my arms are around you." But no rivers of annoyance undermine the arrangements, for they are present as a breakdown of Juan Gris.

The Sonnets is a dream as variously as possible. It lives by its teeth, the most elegant present I could get. The grace and clarity of these poems turn into writing in my skin. Except at night, the only major statement of a blue shirt, such as "these sonnets are an homage to myself, Benjamin Franklin."

When I first read these poems I had a birthday, got married, and told a joke. What else, imitations of Shakespeare? Who can say no to it later? Do I even understand the dark trance of these sonnets? No, for they are present. Trains go by, and they *are* trains, alone in stillness, the code of the west. Any syntactical error of goodbye honors gunfire by Max Jacob. She had a great toe! It hurts on the 15th day of November. But then, a hurting toe is worth at least more or less one apple belly stride toward the sofa of wide melancholy. What these sonnets unclench shall increase from this, returning past the houses he has passed.

Everyday Oops

Slips in the Poetry of Everyday Life

The Poetry of Everyday Life. What does that mean? Does it mean the poetic quality of everyday life or poetry *about* everyday life? I don't know. So I'm going to sidestep this ambiguity by talking about something that happens in everyday life that can lead to poetry and that in fact led to the subject of this talk. When I was invited to speak on the subject of the poetry of everyday life, my mind immediately slipped over to the *psychopathology* of everyday life, the title of Freud's essay that discusses the slip of the tongue.

According to Freud, the slip of the tongue is not just a simple mistake. Like dreams, it is a revelation of a repressed desire, a breakthrough of the unconscious. In other words, the slip of the tongue allows for a fuller expression of the whole self. Freud likens the slip of the tongue to mistakes in reading:

> Both irritating and laughable is a lapse in reading to which I am frequently subject when I walk through the streets of a strange city during my vacation. I then read *antiquities* on every shop sign that shows the slightest resemblance to the word. (*The Basic Writings of Sigmund Freud* [New York: Random House, 1938], 88)

To the slip of the tongue and to misreading I would add mishearing, or slip of the ear. Chronic mishearing can be as-

---

"Everyday Oops" was written in April 1988 as a talk to be delivered at the Poetry Project at St. Mark's Church in New York, as part of the Poetry Project's annual spring symposium, whose theme that year was "The Poetry of Everyday Life."

cribed to partial deafness, but in some cases it is more than
that. It can be selective. My henpecked grandfather misheard
my grandmother when he *wanted* to; that is, when he wanted
to fend her off. For example, if she would say, "Noah, go to the
store right now and buy a gallon of milk," he might answer,
"You want me to buy a gal some milk? What gal?" The novelist
Henry Green seems to have had a similar penchant:

INTERVIEWER: I've heard it remarked that your work is "too
    sophisticated" for American readers, in that it offers no
    scenes of violence—and "too subtle," in that its message is
    somewhat veiled. What do you say?
MR. GREEN: Unlike the wilds of Texas, there is very little vio-
    lence over here. A bit of child-killing of course, but no
    straight shootin'. [. . .]
INTERVIEWER: And how about "subtle"?
MR. GREEN: I don't follow. *Suttee,* as I understand it, is the
    suicide—now forbidden—of a Hindu wife on her husband's
    flaming bier. I don't want my wife to do that when my time
    comes—and with great respect, as I know her, she won't. . . .
INTERVIEWER: I'm sorry, you misheard me; I said "subtle"—
    that the message was too subtle.
MR. GREEN: Oh, *subtle,* how dull!

            (*Paris Review,* no. 19 [Summer 1958]: 64–65)

I suspect that Green, who earlier in the interview had claimed
to be a "trifle hard of hearing," used his disability selectively, in
this case as a "veiled" response to a "dull" question.

    To slips of the tongue, eye, and ear we might add those of
the hand. Blaise Cendrars's poem "Misprints" begins: "Spell-
ing errors and misprints make me happy / Some days I feel
like making them on purpose." Cendrars takes a romantic
poet's pleasure in the typographical error as renegade. Retyp-
ing this talk, instead of "slip of the tongue," I put "*lip* of the
tongue" at one point and "slip of the *gongue*" at another, and
I was tempted to leave them in. I have a particular weakness
for typos that form a new and unexpected meaning. In one
of my poems, I used this type of misprint in some of the
lines:

A rib hung from the marble bust of Robert Burns.
Maurice and Edmund tramped many miles over muddy rods.
They went bathing in the other broth.
Edgar divided the dainties among the fiends.
Maples, hemlocks, and elms grew on Mr. Miller's forearms.

And so on. My tastes for this type of wordplay comes partly from my being influenced by poets such as Frank O'Hara and Kenneth Koch.

When I started thinking about this talk, I was sure that the poetry of what is loosely called the New York School would yield abundant examples of these various types of slips, examples that had either "I mean" (as in "I fell like a god, I mean I *feel* like a god) or "oops" (as in "Hey, does Garcia Lorca have a hymen?—oops, I mean *hyphen!*) or some other form of self-correction. In Bill Berkson and Frank O'Hara's "St. Bridget's Hymn to Willem de Kooning" we find: "I think you are the nuts I mean I think you are nuts." In another poem O'Hara wrote: "I hang from the mistletoe / of surprising indigestion, I mean indiscretion" ("3 Poems about Kenneth Koch"). An example from James Schuyler is: "The sky is pitiless. I beg / your pardon? OK then / the sky is pitted" ("The Dog Wants His Dinner"). In "A Dream" Ted Berrigan did it doubly:

> Love came into my room
> I mean my life
> the shape of a Tomato
> it took over everything
> later:
> Forgive me, René Magritte
> I meant "a rose"

and he reversed the process in "so keep on the ball, buddy, i.e. / I mean 'the button'" ("Tambourine Life"). In "Chinese Creep" Kenward Elmslie wrote: "Thought he said: attack of miasma. / Referring to my asthma." Elmslie calls this his "motor disturbance":

> I can't control my current motor disturbance—so clicky,
>   soppy, so picky—like the one that led me to assume
> "disfunction" was Brooklynese for "wedding"
>   ("Motor Disturbance")

There are also unacknowledged variations on the idea of the slip. In John Ashbery's "Night" "We'll take sides" becomes "We'll make sides"; the word *shells* in "peanut shells" gets divided and expanded into "peanut ship wells"; and what earlier might have been "Into the desert / Sand" becomes "Into the desert / The stand." In O'Hara's "Poem in January" the "buttered bees" probably edged out "buttered peas," and in his "Second Avenue" "the violet waves crested" becomes "the violet waves crusted."

The difficulty of finding these—and other—examples led me to realize that they were only signposts leading to what I shall call the "deeper oops." These deeper oops are part of an aesthetic stance, a level of diction, and an attitude about the self and the presentation of that self in poetry. The aesthetic stance came partly out of surrealism and surrealism's welcoming the unconscious into art. In America of the 1940s and 1950s, surrealism was translated most beautifully into Action Painting, where the controlled accident played such a large role. Poets such as O'Hara and Koch got the excitement of the controlled accident into their work—sometimes through intentional mistranslation—but they rejected many of surrealism's less attractive features: its doctrinaire stridency, its inflated self-importance, its spiderweb creepiness, and ultimately its humorlessness. The down-to-earth tone of some of O'Hara's poems (I'm marvelous and extraordinary, but I do this, I do that, too) reflected this humanized, everyday-Joe surrealism. O'Hara's poetry is often chatty, associative, bold, and fallible. Without being a confessional poet, he's willing to let the reader see when he goes awry, or, rather than erasing the mistake, he uses it to move the poem in a new direction.

Many of James Schuyler's poems are written from the point of view of a guy doing something ordinary like sitting at a window or strolling, and this dailiness is emphasized by sudden changes and veerings due to mistakes: "Smoke streaks, no, / cloud strokes" ("Growing Dark") or

Hamlin Garland rose up from the Oklahoma powwow and
    declared with spirit,
"I will write *The Red Pioneer*. President 'Teddy' Roosevelt shall
    hear,

> I mean, Great Chief, read of the travail of the Polished-Stone-
> Age Aboriginals adapting to the White Man's way.
> How."

Kenneth Koch's long poem *When the Sun Tries to Go On* might be read as one massive slip of the tongue:

> Oh yes, the golf-balls! "We were three golf-balls
> Yesterday until pilgrim milkman rhododendron
> Pansy of navy gorilla

His "Taking a Walk with You" is a brilliant and funny catalog of errors: "I Thought 'muso bello' meant 'Bell Muse'" and "I thought Axel's Castle was a garage." He goes on:

> I misunderstand Renaissance life: I misunderstand:
> The Renaissance;
> Ancient China;
> The Middle Atlantic States and what they are like;
> The tubes of London and what they mean;
> Titian, Michaelangelo, Vermeer;
> The origins of words;
> What others are talking about;
> Music from the beginnings to the present time

Kenward Elmslie's poetry is replete with words that give you the feeling that, in a previous incarnation, they were other words, or that, like enchanted toys, they take on another life as soon as you aren't looking. As he says in "Another Island Groupage," "we ate the Spear People syrup pear / and listened for 'twin' words." By "twin words" he means not only words that rhyme but also those that seem to have some deeper connection (*gismo* and *Quiz Mo*). In "Pavilions" the twin words reverberate back and forth:

> he who is split
> windows in June
> turn to mirrors in Jan
> like milk in mid-air
> windows in Jan
> turn to mirrors in June

At this point the head beings to reel: the slips slipping on each other.

It is interesting that the only book by John Ashbery that openly uses mistakes (*The Tennis Court Oath*) is considered by some to be a mistake itself, the black sheep of his canon.

I realize that, in the course of this talk, the simple idea of the slip of the tongue has brought forth a certain amount of hot air. In such small compass, it's necessary to use abstractions—the New York School, surrealism, the self, aesthetic stance, etc.—without defining them, but I beg your indulgence on the grounds that even this talk is a part of everyday life, oops and all.

New Reading

The twentieth century has changed the way we read, and the change has been relatively abrupt. The proliferation of advertising, the "explosion" of the media, and the influence of modernism in literature have caused us to perceive words in ways foreign to our ancestors. By this I don't mean to trot out the old "what would Aristotle think if he saw computer graphics" type of truism. I mean to suggest that the change goes deeper, that our fundamental sense of what reading is and how to do it has changed.

Imagine that you are driving down a highway and you see, over on the right, the word *GAS* six hundred miles tall. The letters rest lightly on the ground, from where they sweep up through the clouds, their tops disappearing beyond the stratosphere. You would be astonished, like a hillbilly in the 1930s seeing a billboard for the first time. Until then the only words he might have ever seen—perhaps in the Bible—were tiny.

But you are sophisticated. You have seen faces 50 feet tall, moving and talking, as real as life. You are not like 91-year-old Harold Clough who, at his first movie as a boy in rural Vermont around 1912, saw a train heading toward him and got up and ran for his life. You have seen words written in vapor across the sky, you have seen them flow around the tops of buildings like a revolving halo, you have seen them fly toward you in different colors and explode (on TV and in computer games). You've seen them flash on and off, buck like a horse, and spell themselves out in neon script. You've seen them in a hundred different typefaces, big, fat, skinny, curly, leaning, antique, shadowed. You may have seen them deployed in fasci-

From *Creative Reading: What It Is, How to Do It, and Why* (National Council of Teachers of English, 1997).

nating new ways, combined with sound and images, in CD-ROMs.[1] Many of us have experienced these new presentations of words, which might be called the popular side of creative reading. Most of these forms are now so ordinary that we take them for granted.

Less common are the new ways of reading necessitated by modern literature. In 1897, when Stéphane Mallarmé's poem "A Throw of the Dice" was published, the literary page was given a new look: the lines, set in various sizes, were scattered around the page, so that the white space around the words suddenly took on an importance of its own. The poem even called into question whether or not we were to read it one page at a time or across the two-page spread. Christian Morgenstern's poem "Night Song" used symbols instead of alphabetical letters: it didn't need to be translated from the original German. The shaped poetry of the past—in which a poem had the physical shape of its subject matter—experienced a rejuvenation in the hands of Guillaume Apollinaire (see his poem "It's Raining") and helped spawn what became known as "concrete poetry." The Italian Futurist poets espoused a kind of writing they called *parole in libertà,* or "words set loose"; words, sometimes truncated or dislocated, appeared in Cubist collages and paintings. In Switzerland, Germany, and France the Dada poets experimented with chance poetry and sound poetry, as did Kurt Schwitters, the inventor of a one-man art

---

1. At a recent lecture-demonstration by the head of a CD-ROM company, a member of the audience asked a disarming question: "Does anybody actually *read* CD-ROMs?" The implication was that CD-ROMs sometimes have wonderful combinations of graphics, sound, and text but that the text comes in a far distant third. Who would really want to read, for example, *Moby-Dick* from a computer monitor? It's not just that prolonged staring at a cathode-ray tube can make you feel that masonry nails have been driven into your eyes; it's also that the monitor is a glass wall between reader and text, a text that remains distant and cool. Reading a book is more intimate partly because it's more sensuous. You can hold and caress a book, and, when it's new, you can even sniff its heady combination of printer's ink, binding glue, and fresh paper and, when the book grows old, its ineffable essence of library. Books are like food. Will we ever "devour" a CD-ROM? As for reading in bed . . . .

movement, Merz. Apollinaire and Blaise Cendrars brought "found" elements into their poetry, such as the overheard chit-chat in the former's conversation-poem "Monday Rue Christine" and the latter's wonderful plagiarizations in his *Nineteen Elastic Poems* and *Documentaries*. Both poets were also attracted to advertising:

> You read the handbills the catalogs the posters that really sing
> That's poetry and there are newspapers if you want prose this
> morning[2]

Gertrude Stein's experimental repetitions made her prose pieces sound like delirious children's stories. Poets such as e. e. cummings took words apart and put them back together in unusual configurations. James Joyce, in *Finnegans Wake*, let the words run on in a kind of cosmic babble.

Obviously, modern literature has caused us to read in new ways.[3] But older literature does too. It all depends on what we mean by "new." Is it new as in "new to humankind" or new as in "new to me"? For example, is reading e. e. cummings for the first time really any more new than reading Chaucer (in Middle English) for the first time? The main difference between reading contemporary literature and reading classical literature is that the latter has a large body of criticism sur-

---

2. From Apollinaire's poem "Zone," my translation.

3. An awareness of sign language and modern dance can expand our definition of reading. Peter Wisher, a coach and professor of physical education at Gallaudet University (the school for the deaf), created a new form of dance for his students. When viewed by a hearing audience, Wisher's choreography appears simply to include large gestures, but to deaf audiences who know American Sign Language the dance is also operatic, because the dancers are actually signing the lyrics with their entire bodies. Years before I learned of Wisher's choreography, I wrote two pieces that echo it, a poem ("Yak and Yak") and an article ("Phrases in Grammar and Dance"), both reprinted in the present volume. Many choreographers of modern dance are aware of the relationship between dance and language and that in some way, perhaps unconsciously, their dances can be "read." Such relationships have been the subject of study for many years by bee experts such as Karl von Frisch, author of *The Dancing Bees*.

Fig. 2.   Futurist poem by F.T. Marinetti

rounding it, from which we can learn how other people have read it. Contemporary literature has fewer such "support systems." In deciding how to read a piece of writing that is radically new, we have to rely on our own nerve, gut reaction, and sense of what is beautiful and valuable. The more flexible we are in our reading, the more likely we are to be able to "handle" new work. If our literature is to be various and bold, flexibility in the way we read is crucial, because ultimately it is we who decide whether a work becomes part of our literature or just another forgotten book.

Finally, modern experimental literature has not only made us aware that there are many ways to read, but it has also intensified the traditional intimacy of simply reading a book, spending time alone with an author in a quiet corner. As third-grader Namah McKay put it:[4]

Myself!

I love to read,
in a chair,
in a bed,
in a warm blanket,
in front of a fire.
My head is like a library,
with many words and pages.
I like the quietness,
I like the quietness like a gentle breeze,
I am like a lake,
with boats of books
crossing over me.

---

4. Written in a class conducted by poet-teacher Judith Steinbergh.

Camel Serenade

New Computer Writing and Art

The use of the computer in writing is going to be very interesting in the next few years. It is going to be interesting for teachers, who will have better software and new methods to work with, and it will be interesting for writers, who will explore the computer's new artistic possibilities. It will also be interesting for readers, because a new computer art/writing will call forth new ways of "reading."

My own experiences with the computer have lead me to these optimistic predictions. Naive and skeptical, I originally suspected that the personal computer was technology's latest way of entertaining us away from more important things. The "hype" that accompanied the proliferation of the personal computer—"In five years everyone will *have to have a computer to survive*"—made computers sound depressing, enslaving, even tacky. Secretly, though, I was curious to know more about them. As a writer, I was intrigued by the flat, industrial-sounding term *word processing*. Surely they couldn't do to words what they had done to cheese. But how was I going to find out?

The question was answered when the Atari Institute for Action Research donated two Atari 800's to Teachers & Writers Collaborative. Suddenly it became part of my work at T&W to learn about the computer. Before the equipment arrived I started reading computer books and magazines, which got me in the mood, so to speak; but I learned a lot

First published in *Teachers & Writers* 16, no. 3 (January–February 1985), of which, conveniently, I was the editor. It's funny how wrong my optimistic prediction was.

more, and more quickly, through informal instruction from computer people at New York University's Alternative Media Center, who were about to collaborate with Teachers & Writers on school computer projects in writing and graphic art. Using a strictly hands-on method, in a couple of hours they taught me enough elementary word processing so that when I needed to learn more I could usually figure it out by consulting the manual.

Over the next couple of months I came to what appear to be the writer's standard conclusions about word processing. It can be wonderful for writing prose. It allows you to write more volubly and freely, and it makes revisions easy and even entertaining. It eliminates the agony of endless retyping. For poetry—at least the kind of poetry I was interested in writing—it was lousy, partly because of the restricted length of line on the Atari (36 characters), partly because it didn't "feel" right. The monitor, the computer console, the disc drive, the diskettes, the need for electricity, the lack of physical mobility, all these seemed contrary to the free—in every sense of the word—nature of the poetry I wanted to write. Ultimately, though, there was no getting around the fact that my feel for prose, especially expository prose, had improved.

Summer came. I retreated to the hills of northern Vermont, taking an Atari with me. It was there that my view of the computer widened more dramatically. Through my son Wayne, who for the past few years had been discreetly spending time in video arcades, I fell under the spell of video games. When video games are good they are *very* good. (After one particularly feverish, obsessive night of playing Crossfire until five A.M., I developed an alarming case of joystick thumb.) It was also through my son, though, that I was initiated into the mysteries of programming. Not only had he been playing Wizard of War in the arcades, he had also been learning programming in school.

I couldn't let him get "ahead" of me, so I began Atari's self-tutorial program in BASIC. When I wasn't sure about some point or other, Wayne explained. He found the "bugs" in my exercise programs. Although not a sophisticated programmer, he pointed out some slicker programming techniques. Without meaning to, he showed me that he was no longer the little boy who needed his father's help: the tables had turned. I felt a strange new respect for him as a young man.

I already respected his artistic ability. Since the age of three he had created imaginative poems, stories, drawings, and cartoons. Now, with the computer, he began to write programs that produced graphic and sometimes witty results on the screen. One night, just before we were to have dinner with our neighbor Joe, he quickly wrote a program that produced the flashing yellow word *JOE'S,* with an animated arrow, like a diner sign, pointing in the direction of Joe's house. After a certain number of flashes, a siren began to wail, the screen went dark, and the words "It's a raid!" appeared.

Over the next few weeks I meddled in his computer doodlings. One day I walked by the computer and saw on the screen an Egyptian pyramid that kept hypnotically reappearing in changing colors: it was like a visual song in the mind of a desert animal. I said to Wayne, "Put CAMEL SERENADE at the bottom." He did, so that it appeared one letter at a time, coinciding with each new pyramid: *C, CA, CAM, CAME, CAMEL,* etc. The slow, rhythmical appearance of the letters suggested not only the camel's gait but also brought forth associations with the words inside *camel* and *serenade: C* suggested *see, CA* suggested *California, CAM* suggested a machine with parts moving at measured intervals, *CAME* suggested "arrived," and so on, with a particularly pretty suggestion that the camel is named Serena. Of course I had none of this in mind when I asked him to add CAMEL SERENADE to his graphics.

Over the next few weeks we came up with some funny and serious and beautiful little works, many of which involved visual images, sound, words, and motion. Sometimes, just to see what would happen, we borrowed commands from programs in books we didn't even understand. These new works were a cross between poetry, graphic design, and animated cartoons. I had never seen anything quite like them.

Wayne created his final masterpiece of the summer by parodying a portion of Atari's program for the BASIC self-tutorial course. He listed the program and then creatively revised it. Where the program had asked questions such as "What is the correct command for printing 'hello'?" he had it ask ridiculous questions, such as "What is the correct command for Jack

Lord's hair?" (he was an ironic fan of "Hawaii Five-O" reruns). Where the Atari program had some little computer musical motif, he put a wild selection from Japan, a New Wave rock group. The resulting scramble—a completely insane tutorial program that no one could possibly follow—was a wonderful dadaist parody.

In the meantime we had begun to work on a pilot project that had been floating around in my fantasies for the past year or so. I had been dreaming of creating writing games for the computer, games that would be as much fun as Crossfire and at the same time as true as possible to my experience of writing creatively. In a couple of weeks we roughed out a first version of one of these games.

To create the kinds of art works Wayne did on the computer you have to know how to do some programming. Very few of the poets and novelists I know—mostly thirty and over—know how to program. If they use the computer, it is for word processing only. Over the new few years, though, there will be more and more creative kids coming out of school with the ability both to program and to write creatively, and when that happens we will begin to see imaginative computer artworks for which we have as yet no name.

Essays on Teaching Writing

Phrases in Grammar and Dance

I've always liked prepositional phrases. In school it was relatively easy for me to learn what they were and to diagram them. In the house. Under the bed. Over the rainbow. There were no horrible complications of voice, mood, or agreement. And the diagrammatic structure for prepositional phrases was so crisp and neat: a line slanting down to the right, then turning to run horizontally.

I think that when I was first taught diagramming, in the seventh or eighth grade, this graphic depiction caused me to associate prepositional phrases and human arms (or legs): the preposition was the upper arm (or leg above the knee), the noun object the forearm (or leg below the knee). In fact, it was as if an entire sentence, its structure laid bare in diagramming, mirrored the human body. The subject corresponded to the head, the predicate to the trunk, the arms and legs to prepositional phrases. (I can't remember if I extended the comparison as far as conjunctions/genitals, though, given my willingness at thirteen to see sexual connotations in everything, it's possible that I did. I'm sure I dimly felt the main clause to be male, the dependent clause female.) Such associations have a visual as well as psychological basis: relating sentence diagramming to the human body came naturally—after learning to draw the traditional stick figure.

"Phrases in Grammar and Dance" grew out of a visit to a Brooklyn elementary school to observe dancer/choreographer Andrea Sherman working with children. It appeared in *Teachers & Writers* 18, no. 1 (September–October 1986).

Prepositional phrases still not only remind me of arms and legs, they also give me a visceral sensation of motion, at least when they're concrete. "Under the ground" drives me lower, "across the river" whizzes me forward, "in the sky" elevates me—and not only because of content. *Under* has a Germanic sound that seems to attract other such sounds, gutteral and heavy. The two syllables of *across* are like the two steps for shooting a projectile: the first syllable cocks the mechanism, the second is the sound of the projectile whizzing through the air. *In* is so small a word as to be lighter than air, calling forth other airy sounds, clusters of helium balloons.

The physiology of uttering these three prepositions re-inforces their respective impressions. Say them aloud now: *under, across, in. Under* begins low in the throat and ends by being pressed down by the tongue and lips. *Across* begins in the back of the mouth and then is hissed outward into the air. The short *i* of *in* rises to the long (and "high") *i* sound in *sky:* it rises. Perhaps this is why the image of balloons came to mind a few sentences back.

In any case, such concrete prepositional phrases make me feel—perhaps where mind and body meet—the actual motion suggested by the phrases. Combined with appropriate rhythms, these phrases become powerful vehicles: by the time we get to "we go" in "Over the river and through the woods to grandmother's house we go," I've already gone!

The movement inherent in concrete prepositional phrases can be seen by contrasting them with abstract ones. "In this case," "of the agreement," "in my opinion" have rhythm (as any words do), but they are static. They are plunked right down where they are. Perhaps this is why people who wish to appear dignified, firm, and stately overuse such phrases. Built into their usage is the prejudice that to move one's body quickly is usually to appear juvenile. Children run and jump. Heads of state move with studied slowness. Middle-aged people seek youthfulness by jumping about in aerobics classes. I jump around on a tennis court. No wonder we get drowsy and doze when hearing a talk bogged down in phrases like "under consideration," "in deliberation," and "of achievement." An old meaning of *abstract* is, after all, "absent in mind."

Of course abstraction has its uses. The unfortunate thing about abstraction is that its *abuses* don't lead to anything beautiful or interesting. For example, disorganized strings of concrete phrases can be wonderfully ludicrous, as in "The Browns returned this morning from their vacation in the mountains on a bus," in which the suddenly miniature Browns spend their leisure time amidst the little mountains situated atop a bus. In this example the scale of things fluctuates wildly, releasing a surrealistic humor. By seeing the imaginative possibilities in such ludicrousness, creative writers can use confused strings of prepositional phrases to good advantage.

I've always been attracted to the lankiness of long strings of prepositional phrases: "in the city of Cincinnati under an enormous elm in the summer of 1942 . . . ." This series of phrases generously opens up and extends itself, like a carpenter's rule. It has a midsummer sense of timelessness built into its syntax. It exudes ease and flow and relaxation, something like the rhythm of using the extra *and* in the first half of this very sentence. Carried to extremes, such lankiness can create elongations that, like Giacometti sculptures, instill in us a new but oddly familiar mood: "in the light of the moon in my bed at midnight in the late summer in Oslo." Pushed far enough, some mysterious or at least amusing image emerges, not despite the confusion, but because of it. The moon gets in bed with you.

Other types of phrases—verb phrases, participial, gerundive, and infinitive phrases—don't have for me the strong physiological associations that prepositional phrases do. Verb phrases are really just verbs, no? Participial phrases are perpetual motion machines: the *-ing* keeps them going forever. Gerund phrases are perpetual motion machines that stopped and became frozen in noun form. Infinitive phrases are Platonic versions of verbs and their accoutrements. Also, these all lack the attractive simplicity and particularity of direction of prepositional phrases.

A phrase of an entirely different order, the dangling

phrase, sometimes has a comic effect similar to that of the misplaced prepositional phrase, as in "Being in a hurry to leave Denver, the dented fender was not repaired then." Dangling phrases are reminiscent of the comic dislocations of what the Germans called *Grotesktanz,* or "eccentric dancing," and of the consciously misplaced and witty phrases of contemporary dance choreography.

So much for the confused, misplaced, comic, or surreal phrase. What about the graceful, articulate, adroit use of phrases? What about the periodic sentence that flows from beginning to end like a big river? Is it not related to the classical ballet, its nineteenth-century counterpart?

The graceful dancer has (too) often been described as "poetry in motion." This is flattering to the dancer, at the expense of poetry, for what it overlooks is that poetry already has motion. It does, though, refer to the relation we feel between poetry and dance. The phrase in writing and the phrase in dance don't seem all that different to me. Given the somewhat grammatical structure of dance and the kinetic nature of syntax, it might be useful to see how they could strengthen and develop each other (something like the "body syntonicity" Seymour Papert discusses in his book *Mindstorms*).

Here are some classroom exercises toward that end:

1A. Have each student invent a dance phrase: a brief gesture or movement of any type, using any part(s) of the body.
1B. Then have the student write down a prepositional phrase suggested by the dance phrase.

   Note: Prepositions involving directions (*behind, under, through, around,* etc.) are the most physical. For example, a student whose dance phrase involves taking a backward step might write the corresponding "behind the bear."
2. Do the same as in 1 but reverse the order: prepositional phrases first, dance versions of them second.

   Note: "Abstract" prepositions (*of, at, by, for,* etc.) are more challenging to translate into dance phrases.
3. Have three or four students perform their dance phrases at the front of the class, as their classmates "read" them from left to right and translate them into prepositional phrases that read consecutively.

4. Same as above, only reverse the order: have students read aloud a string of three or four prepositional phrases and have a corresponding three or four students at the front spontaneously translate them into dance phrases.

Gimmicks

The word *gimmick* has derogatory connotations. It suggests something cheap, tricky, fast, without substance, even immoral. There are intelligent people who attack the use of gimmicks or devices in teaching imaginative writing, on the grounds that such devices encourage kids to be thoughtless smart alecks, witty at the expense of substance, satisfied with a glib surface but insensitive to depth of feeling. Such critics usually emphasize the importance of meaning.

Were there a School of Gimmicks, its members might retort that the Defenders of Meaningfulness tend to be boring creeps who confuse self-expression with value, that the most sincere statement of feeling is no better than any other sincere statement, that what makes the difference in creative expression is style. In other words, concern yourself with style, and everything else will take care of itself. These are two extreme points of view, of course, rehashings of the old conflict between those who favor Form and those who favor Content in literature.

The fact is that there is no appreciable difference between a teacher who uses gimmicks with intelligence and one who

---

"Gimmicks" is from *The Whole Word Catalogue 2,* edited by Bill Zavatsky and me and published in 1977 by McGraw-Hill / Teachers & Writers Collaborative. In this piece I summarized eleven writing ideas I had used, among others, in teaching imaginative writing to elementary school children at P.S. 61 in New York, in a program sponsored by Teachers & Writers Collaborative, around 1971. Some of the ideas later became commonplace in classrooms around the country, but in the early days of poets-in-the-schools they seemed innovative.

emphasizes meaning with intelligence. A heartless use of gimmicks will produce worn-out surrealist imitations; a narrow insistence on self-expression will produce baloney.

Self-expression is therapeutic and flashy technique is entertaining, but neither is necessarily good writing. So don't let anyone hornswoggle you into thinking you should teach one to the exclusion or detriment of the other.

Found Poems

The "found poem" has thrown some intellectual monkey wrenches into modern literature and few people seem to want to deal with their implications. It is okay to bring a piece of driftwood into a high school art class and declare it a "found sculpture," and it is okay for a Pop artist to paint a Campbell's soup can or incorporate everyday objects into assemblages, but it is not yet acceptable to appropriate, say, a New York Yankees baseball game as an art event or conceptual artwork. The notion of originality in art, which became so attractive with the Romantic poets and artists, needs to be reexamined, to see exactly what is meant. Poets such as John Giorno, who has written all his poetry for the past ten or so years using nothing but found words, might argue that almost all words are found anyway. The subject is too large and probably too boring to be dealt with here.

So, how to proceed in the classroom? Have each kid select a passage from a book, newspaper, or conversation, write it down as if it were a poem, give it a title (which they might also find), and read it aloud. If you have a lot of different materials available to the kids, the range of poems will be wider and more interesting. Some will seem quite good, others will flop. You might ask the kids why some found poems work better than others.

You might also discuss how context changes words. A paragraph in a news story will change if it is removed from the story and read separate from it. The words are the same, but the different context makes the tone different. Something very sad in a story might be very funny when removed from the story and read to someone who did not know the origin of the piece.

You might feel sorry for a blind person making his way down the street, but if you saw the same person standing before a sunset over the Grand Canyon, you would be astonished and, perhaps, filled with curiosity about this intriguing individual. His context (street, Grand Canyon) has changed the way you feel about him.

Here are two examples of found poems by two modern masters of the genre, John Giorno and Charles Reznikoff.

> An unemployed
> machinist
> An unemployed machinist
> who travelled
> here
> who travelled here
> from Georgia
> from Georgia 10 days ago
> 10 days ago
> and could not find
> a job
> and could not find a job
> walked
> into a police station
> walked into a police station
> yesterday and said
> yesterday
> and said:
>
> "I'm tired
> of being scared
> I'm tired of being scared."

(John Giorno, from *Balling Buddha* [Kulchur Foundation])

Giorno's poem, which is probably taken from a newspaper article, gains power by a skillful use of repetition. In the following poem Charles Reznikoff has also drawn on public documents, in this case from court records of the period 1885–90, for his long poem *Testimony* (published in paperback by New Directions):

It got to be past ten o'clock at night.
Mr. Stokes read the papers over and over again.
Finally he said: "Don't you think I ought to take more time?"

Mr. Siren replied: "You are a businessman, Mr. Stokes
and you understand this paper, don't you?"

"Yes."
"And you understand *this* paper, don't you?"
But Mr. Stokes sat there with the pen in in his hand and kept
    hesitating.

Then Mr. Siren said: "Come, Stokes, if you understand it,
    sign it."
"I guess I had better take more time to look it over."
"If you put it off,
you will be no nearer tomorrow.
Come on and sign it.
Sign it, Sign it!"

Marcel Duchamp, who was probably the first to raise this art form above the level of the joke, also legitimized the doctoring of the found object. He would make small but powerful alterations of the original material. Here, for instance, is a doctored found poem (although not by Duchamp):

> One of the victims
> of that terrible accident
> last August 17
> was a Bronx woman
> whose right leg was
> made entirely of diamonds

where the last line is a substitute for the word *severed*.

An interesting variation, one that Giorno has explored, is to bring together found material from different sources, placing them one after the other, sometimes in a sort of weave that makes the disparate pieces relate to one another, and to create a new context that has little to do with their original ones.

Challenge Verse

A Penguin book called *Poems from the Sanskrit* (translated with an introduction by John Brough, 1968) tells us how Indian writers would sometimes challenge each other in writing by providing each other with the last line of a poem, asking the friend to write the poem to go before it. The challenge consisted in making the last line so outrageous that it would require mental gymnastics to figure out what might come before. The procedure is more interesting than the one that suggests a given opening line (such as "One day when I was walking home from school . . ."). I gave my sixth-graders at P.S. 61 in New York the final line ("And the hippos were boiled in their tanks") and had them write poems that ended with it. The particular class had a lot of experience in writing poetry, so they had no trouble leading up to this ridiculous conclusion. Examples:

> And the elephants turned pink like strawberries.
> And the stars came falling by thousands.
> And the hippos were boiled in their tanks.
>
> (Vivien Tuft)

> The hippos were there,
> just minding their own business,
> when suddenly they were boiling.
> They felt like a teabag in a teapot.
> They tried very hard to get out but failed,
> and the hippos were boiled in their tanks.
>
> (Jeannie Turner)

I then asked kids to make up their own outrageous final line, or to make up one and trade it with a friend, then fill in the poem before. Examples:

> There was a fire and my dream caught on fire and
> then the hippos were boiled in my dreams. There
> was a fire and my dream caught on fire and then
> the hippos were boiled in my dream.
>
> (Guy Peters)

I had a race with a centipede
and it was very fast
but when I won the race
the centipede's feet flew off.

(Oscar Marcilla)

The square rabbits lay sitting
in the hay (that was burning)

The round salamanders lay changing
to a dim black

And the hippos were boiled
in their tanks.

And the pizza was stuck in the cave
forever.

The spaghetti was steaming hot

the sauce burned my tongue

and the pizza was stuck in the cave
forever.

(Tracy Roberts)

I dreamed a beautiful dream
that the hippos were drowned in whipped cream.

(Miklos Lengyel)

The inky paper stinked
and I started to play the violin
My big purple-orange feet hurt in my shoes
and I put my name in a pot of nuts

(Lisa Smalley and Tracy Roberts)

Explosions

Kids seem to like it when things are decimated. A child will
patiently build an entire town of blocks for the ultimate plea-
sure of demolishing it in a single devastating attack. Everyone
has lined up dominoes only to watch them topple in chain
reaction. Hence, it's a natural to have your kids write about

what happens when various things explode. Be sure that they pick some unconventional things for explosions, not just bombs. Examples:

The Now Explosions

Popcorn explodes like an earthquake
Coffee explodes and smells like firecrackers
Gunpowder explodes and smells like a match
When an oilwell explodes
Whoever got hit by it explodes
An oil tank explodes like a stove
A rocket explodes like a balloon
A garbage can explodes when there's too much garbage in it
A notebook explodes when there's too much paper in it
A black board explodes when there's too many words on it
A classroom explodes
When there are too many kids in it

(Lorraine Fedison)

When we go into the music room
instruments explode

When we hear Rock & Roll
We explode and can't control ourselves

(Jorge Robles)

Mistakes

An entertaining way to teach correct language is to have kids indulge themselves in error, using as many incorrect grammatical forms as they can. The following example, from *The Old Farmer's 1975 Almanac* by Robert B. Thomas, is a little anthology of mistakes:

Each pronoun agrees with their antecedent. Just between you and I, case is important. Verbs has to agree with their subjects. Watch out for irregular verbs which has cropped into our language. Don't use no double negatives. A writer mustn't shift your point of view. When dangling, don't use participles. Join clauses good, like a conjunction should. Don't use a run-on sentence you got to punctuate it. About sentence fragments. In letters themes reports articles and stuff like that we use commas to keep a string of items apart. Don't use commas, which aren't necessary. It's important to use apostrophe's right. Don't abbrev. Check to see if you any words out. In my opinion I think that an author when he is writing shouldn't get into the habit of making use of too many unnecessary words that he does not really need. And, of course, there's that old one: Never use a preposition to end a sentence with. Last but not least, lay off clichés.

You should point out to your kids that mistakes can lead to interesting new discoveries, as with the case of Kenneth Koch's student who wrote "swan of bees" instead of "swarm of bees."

The Blackboard

It is often surprising for a poet to realize that kids in many classrooms feel that the blackboard is off-limits to them unless they are supposed to be there. The old idea of the grumpy teacher entering the classroom only to find the drawing of an ugly person on the board, with the word *techur* next to it, suggests that this is a widespread situation: guerrilla attacks on the board must be furtive, and they are almost always political or social, involving control of the media and commentary on social behavior (X loves Y). Sometimes the graffiti are naughty or pornographic. In these cases the board is a reserved precinct that contains "enemy" information (homework assignments, "school" stuff, the date, lesson plans), the enemy being the Teacher as Power Figure, and the weaker person's response is often to strike back when he or she has the chance. This attempt at self-expression is healthy, although childish. A more civilized and direct form of exchange might take place if the kids were given an area of the board, or given the entire board part of the day (or week). It is not suggested here that students and teacher become indistinguishable, but that the useless exercise of prerogative be abandoned because it is destructive to a healthy relationship.

Question Marks and Exclamation Points

An interesting experiment you might try with your kids involves changing declarative sentences into questions and exclamations.

> In the beginning God created the heavens and the earth!
>
> Do I pledge allegiance to the flag of the United States of America?
>
> Is April the cruellest month?
>
> Did she sing beyond the genius of the sea?
>
> Have I eaten the plums that were in the icebox?

And so on!

I'll Never Tell You

Have the kids write a poem beginning "I'll never tell you . . . ." It's interesting to see how different kids take this idea. Some will actually tell you things that previously they were shy about saying. Others will toy with you, giving hints of some secret. Some will feel they have some secret that is untellable, even anonymously. This kind of poem will at least introduce the idea that writers withhold as much or more than they say and that what is left out is often as important as what is put in.

Examples:

> I'll never tell you.
> I just can't tell you.
> I just can't, but can't tell you.
> That I hate writing this.
>
> There I just told you.
>
> Ain't I stupid, I just told you.
>
> But then, I can't tell you.
> I just can't.
> I really can't.

>   *

I'll never tell anybody that almost all of
the kids in the class think I'm their friend
but I'm not.

*

I'll never tell you that you are a duck.

*

I know a secret!
I know a secret!

　　Ha, Ha, Ha
　　I'll never tell you. . . . . .
　　that. . . . .

　　　　*

I'll never tell you that I have a date
with? 6-1 He He Heh Ha Ha Haw How Ha

　　*

Miss Pitts gives me dirty assignments
in muddy classroom. Ha Ha Hee Hee
Haa Ha Ha Ha Haw
That I died in a coma
That I will get married in church
with?

That my new name is?

That I have an excellent personality
And Do Not Read This Letter If You Do

I'll get Hercules and tear gas bombs.

Pronoun-Who Poems

This is a poem that derives purely from an interest in a
particular grammatical form. Have the kids write lines begin-
ning with pronouns (*I, you, he, she, it, we, they*) and with the
word *who* in the middle of the sentence. For instance, "I am
the man who wrote this sentence. You are the person who
reads it. He is the one who saw you reading it. She is the one
who asked what you were doing. It was the sentence who said

just one thing. We are the morons who didn't understand. They are the geniuses who explained it to us." (Obviously this example takes a funny jump in the *it* line.) Some examples from sixth-graders:

> I am the monster who owns mice.
> You are the mouse who is owned by the monster.
> He is the chick who is owned by the monster.
> She is the mother who owns the monster.
> It is the brother who sees the monster often.
> We are the family who is full of monsters.
> They are the family who owns mice and a chicken.
>
> (Oscar Marcilla)

I Who Know

> They who call me Vivien don't know my real name.
> He, she, me and myself really know.
> I who never tell hide behind a black magic curtain
> And say to everybody,
> "My name is a weird one
> And it lies ahead in the never never land in Holland
> On a big mountain hidden in the snow."
>
> (Vivien Tuft)

Why & Because

Have each student fold a piece of paper across the middle. On the top half have each one write a question beginning with *Why* and on the bottom half an answer beginning with *Because*.

Any question is okay, but the procedure works better if the kids are encouraged to ask interesting or amazing questions or questions they've always wondered about. Naturally many of these questions will be unanswerable ("Why are there two sexes instead of three or four?"). In such cases tell the kids that their Because answers can be guesses, that they needn't worry about giving the "right" answers to their Why questions.

When everyone's finished, have the kids tear their papers along the fold, separating Why and Because, and hand in their Whys first, then their Becauses. Make a stack of Why questions and another stack of Because answers. Shuffle each stack separately. Now, with the stacks side by side, read the question on top of the Whys and the answer on top of the Becauses. Continue to read off the new pairs of questions and answers.

In some cases the results will be utter duds, but others will make a weird or poetic sense. Ask the kids how the answers could be considered good ones. Even the most irrelevant answer can be related to a question.

A variation is for you to think of a Because answer. Remember it. Ask a kid to ask you a Why question, and, when he or she does, give your preconceived answer.

Any kind of compound linguistic structure can be adapted to this process, such as If You / Be Sure, in which the kids give advice, such as "If you come to school / Be sure to bring your brain" or "If you are a girl / Be sure to stand up for your rights." Now, just mixing these two examples, we get, "If you come to school, be sure to stand up for your rights" and "If you are a girl, be sure to bring your brain."

Besides strengthening the students' sense of compound sentences and conditional clauses, the If You / Be Sure form alerts them to didacticism in writing. They will be more aware of advice as a form (moral of the story, sermon, etc.).

Both Why & Because and If You / Be Sure are also good for introducing a discussion of non sequitur and logical paragraph structuring in expository prose. They are also useful for talking about how some things work and others don't and to show how we don't have to understand something to have it strike us as funny.

Telepathic Poems

One teacher suggested a writing idea that I find interesting, though perhaps too bizarre for others. It consists of a sort of experiment in mental telepathy. Here is one way to do it.

Each child chooses or is given a partner. One of them is the "sender," the other is the "receiver." The senders thinks of an image, a line or a sentence, and writes it on his paper, so that his partner cannot see it. The sender then concentrates very hard on the thing he has written, either looking into the receiver's eyes or with eyes closed. The receiver keeps his mind open to receiving the transmission. If something "pops" into his mind, he writes it down, so that the sender can't see it. Then the sender comes up with a second thing to transmit, preferably something that goes with the first he sent, and the receiver writes down what he thinks the second message is, again preferably something to do with the first thing he received. And so on until the participants feel the poem has ended.

Apparently some interesting situations develop: some kids are amazed at how well they receive messages, others find themselves staring into the eyes of one of their classmates for the first time. The situation can extend to discussions that normally do not take place in school. An interested science teacher might coordinate his curriculum to include a study of J. B. Rhine's work (for example, *The Reach of the Mind*) or Peter Tompkins and Christopher Bird's work (*The Secret Life of Plants*).

It goes without saying that this type of study is not intended to encourage occultism for its own sake but, rather, to alert the children to a wider range of possibilities in thinking and writing than they might have hitherto imagined.

I Remember

Many kids who would be thrilled to take a ride in a time machine will also be surprised to learn that they can do just that, in one direction, at least. They can take a ride on their memory back into the past. Remembering (or forgetting) is something we do naturally; we just do it. We feel that some people have good memories and others don't, and we leave it at that. The fact is, our memories can be brought to light better if we learn how to do it. I'm not talking about memory systems that teach you to recite the New York phone book. I mean learning to concentrate and keep your attention on things that happened to you. There are books that deal with this subject with far greater authority and intelligence than I can muster, but I forget their titles. Just kidding! One is *The Art of Memory* by Frances Yates.

But whether or not you're an expert on the subject of memory, you'll find that by simply training your attention on places, events, people, etc. of the past, your memory will begin to give you more of its dim and hidden treasures, sometimes with such detail, clarity, and power that you momentarily have the impression that you have revisited the past.

The artist Joe Brainard invented a new poetic form with his book *I Remember*. He began each entry with "I remember . . ." and wrote down anything that seemed interesting or important, in no particular chronological order. Here are some examples of his work:

> I remember painting "I HATE TED BERRIGAN" in big black letters all over my white wall.

> I remember throwing my eyeglasses into the ocean off the Staten Island Ferry one black night in a fit of drama and depression.

> I remember once when I made scratches on my face with my fingernails so people would ask me what happened, and I would say a cat did it, and, of course, they would know that a cat did not do it.

> I remember the linoleum floors of my Dayton, Ohio room. A white puffy floral design on dark red.

> I remember sack dresses.

> I remember when a fish-tail dress I designed was published in "Katy Keene" comics.

The Care and Feeding of a
Child's Imagination

I started teaching poetry writing at P.S. 61, an elementary school in New York City, at the invitation of Kenneth Koch, the poet whose work there has been presented in his book Wishes, Lies, and Dreams. *The program was sponsored by Teachers & Writers Collaborative, a non-profit group that sends writers into schools to develop new ways of teaching writing. As a hand-to-mouth poet who had never taught, I thought the job sounded challenging but would give me time to write poetry and live my private life. However, as I worked with many different children, I became impressed with the beneficial effects poetry writing was having on their private and social selves. I felt I was being given a rare opportunity for a poet in the twentieth century—to be directly useful to society without compromising myself.*

I still find it hard to recognize myself when the teacher introduces me formally to the class as "Mr. Padgett, the poet who is visiting us today. . . ." I feel dazed as I walk to the blackboard, draw an oval shape on it, and say, to a group of seventh graders, "This is you." They giggle. "I mean, this is a blob. . . ." More giggles. "Let this blob represent the you that is your imagination, your personality, your mind, your Self, whatever there would be left if your body disappeared." I write the number 24 above it to represent one day and draw a line through the blob to mark off 8 hours for sleep. Point-

---

"The Care and Feeding of a Child's Imagination" was written at the invitation of Phyllis Rosser, an editor at *Ms.* magazine, where it appeared, in the May 1976 issue. Although the piece is a hymn to the pleasures of imaginative writing, it takes a negative turn at the very end, an unfortunate attempt on my part to make the piece acceptable to what I imagined to be the *Ms.* audience.

ing to the 16-hour part, I say, "This represents your mental self in the awake state, the you that is here right now. Most people think this part is the whole story. But when you lie down and go to sleep at night, your mind keeps on working, just differently, and sometimes very odd things happen in it." (By now the kids see me zeroing in on the dream-mind.) "This other part of the mind interests me a lot. When I was little I hated to go to sleep, but now I love it, because I'm curious to see what's happening over in that mysterious part of my mind. Last night, for instance, I dreamed . . ." and I go on to recount last night's sleep extravaganza. By the time I'm finished, hands are up, kids anxious to tell me about their favorite dreams or nightmares, dreams that are repeated or continued the next night, funny dreams, romantic dreams, or how you can be in a dream and outside it at the same time. Then I ask, "Were you ever in a car, or a room, or outdoors, and suddenly you have this creepy feeling, that this has all happened exactly the same, sometime before?" Some gasp. Fifteen minutes ago we were total strangers. Now they are really excited about their own personal mysterious, imaginative experiences.

I ask everyone to write down either a dream or a déjà vu experience, being as specific as they can in their descriptions. Not "a monster chased me," but "a green man with fiery pink hair all over his body walked toward me." No, they needn't sign their papers, and, no, don't worry about spelling or grammar. This is not a test. A few kids complain, "I never remember my dreams." I whisper, "Make up something that sounds like a dream." Often they will go on to write about an actual dream they were hesitant to acknowledge. Others respond to "Remember a scary dream you had when you were little."

I read their dream writings aloud, including my own and the regular teacher's. Suddenly the room is filled with a sampling of the classroom unconscious. The anonymity adds to the fascination.

Dream Poem

I dreamed I was in a gigantic room. Everything was made of tiles, the walls, floors, everything. The only piece of furniture was a gold throne. I thought to myself, "What am I doing here? Oh well, I'll sit down." Then all of a sudden the left and right corners of the room opened. I could see beams of light coming in the corners. Very strong light and I could hear cheering. I stood up and a big dinosaur ran through the corner of light. I screamed and ran out the opposite beam of light and fell on a cloud that had sand particles on it. Then I dreamed I fell asleep. I've had this dream 4 times.

(Christine Riblett)

I suggest they keep a diary of their dream lives that they can use as a basis for short stories, fantasy tales, or science fiction. (I've found it helps to replay details from my dreams before I open my eyes in the morning and then write them down immediately.)

Because my basic interest is in creative writing, I encourage kids to say whatever they want, no matter how wacky, weird, or unconventional, and to forgo, if they wish, rules of spelling, grammar, rhyme, and meter. They also have the freedom to write anonymously (until they feel confident enough to sign their work). Kids who have a terrible time spelling simple words naturally dislike writing but are often good storytellers. I take dictation from them, either individually or as a group. I don't want poetry writing to be confused with "schoolwork."

I am not, however, an "anything goes" type. I discourage personal viciousness and constant use of obscenity in writing. Doubtless therapeutic for some, they disconnect most children from their larger, more interesting selves.

I also discourage the kind of competitiveness that makes most kids feel anxious, unloved, and defeated, or vainly victorious: I do not single out the "best" works. Creativity should not be turned into a contest. I let kids talk while they work, move around the room, share ideas, copy from each other (if they feel they must), in short, behave in any way that isn't damaging to the group or to themselves. I encourage them to pay attention to their ideas, to take themselves seriously, even if what they're writing is funny, so that they know that the content of their fantasies is not only acceptable, it is welcome.

A crucial moment for emphasizing this comes when I read the poems aloud. I pause to comment on things I like, as much with my tone of voice as with outright remarks. In fact I praise the poems like mad. Praise makes the kids feel good about what they've done; they've gone out on a limb in their writing, and by damn it worked, somebody liked it! Gradually they gain the self-confidence to write as well as they always could have, with greater ease, pleasure, and satisfaction. They come to appreciate their imaginations, and from there the imaginative lives of others.

By "imaginative lives" I don't mean just the world of the unconscious. One poetry idea called variously Here and Now, Right Now, or Poem of the Senses has the kids focus their attention on the immediate present. In order to present the Right Now idea I secretly study the walls, ceiling, desks, view outside, details of clothes, and gestures that stand out a little, while the teacher introduces me. "This room is very interesting," I begin. "Look at that crack on the wall: it looks like a bolt of lightning. The reflection on the clock face forms a bent shiny rectangle. A yellow pencil is lying on the floor pointing to a red tennis shoe that goes up and down. Do you hear that humming? I feel a little cool breeze on my face as I walk back and forth, and I feel my heart beating in my chest. Do you feel yours? I feel my throat vibrating as I talk. I don't smell anything." Laughter.

"Right now this room is the way it never was before and never will be again because tiny details are constantly shifting." I hold up a piece of chalk and let it drop onto the floor, where it leaves a small bite of chalk. "That chalk falling is now three seconds into the past. Now . . . it's six seconds into the past. . . . What I'd like you all to do is to blot out the past and future. Make yourself one big receiver of impressions: notice what you see, hear, feel (touch), smell, and sense right now. This can be outside your body and mind, like the light powder on the chalkboard; or inside, such as feeling your lungs fill with air or sensing an idea happening in your mind. Make a list—in sentences—of things you never noticed before or things you think no one else will notice. Not boring stuff like 'I see a wall,' but clear details, such as 'There are thousands of little holes in the green cinder blocks, each casting a shadow.'

Or say what it reminds you of: 'The Vietnamese landscape is pitted with shell holes.' "

To make things easier I write on the board:

I see	I feel	I believe
I hear	I think	I imagine
I taste	I sense	I wonder
I smell	I know	etc.

The kids start craning their necks. Consciously focusing on details in the room is peculiar for them but exhilarating.

> I see the dark mouth of a cave.
> I hear the shouts of millions.
> I feel high.
> I think I am getting drunk off this class.
> I smell a blue sea.
> I imagine I am flying.
> I know I am mad.
>
> (Todd Robeson)

This type of poem also shows how repetition is a good substitute for rhyme and meter in teaching poetry to children because it creates a poetic structure without inhibiting their freedom of expression.

Actual events become dreamlike when they sink into the past. "Wouldn't it be great if you could get in a time machine and go back into the past?" I ask one class. "To see George Washington remove his false teeth or Christ right up there on the Cross, a prehistoric man learning how to make fire, the real live Cleopatra, the Titanic sinking. . . . Or into the future. What would we look like? Would we live in plastic bubbles? Hmm. As far as I know, we can't get into the future, but we can travel back into the past by using our own personal time machines, our memories."

I talk about how odd it is to have something on the tip of one's tongue, how wonderful it is to remember something beautiful and valuable that happened to you, how dim and dreamy to remember back to the age of three, or two. . . . If only we could remember how it was before we were born! Finally I say that today I want everyone to get into their own time machines and travel back to something they remember from long ago. It doesn't have to be an earthshaking story, but it should be as specific as possible, recalling colors and details. I tell them to start each story with "I remember. . . ."

I remember when my sister was two, it was her birthday and we went shopping to get a cake at Pathmark. We had to wait on line for about 2 hours and when we got home my mother found out that my sister was sitting on the cake the whole time.

(Carl Johnson)

I remember when I was 3 or 4 my father was very mad at a '59 Ford and so mad he threw the keys at it and busted the ring and the keys went flying in the air and he came inside and mowed over everything and anything including me and he blamed me for it. It took us 3 hours to find 20 keys and we still didn't find one key, the key to the car.

(Tom P.)

Dream Poems, Here and Now Poems, I Remember—these depend directly on the personal experiences of the writers. There are other poetry ideas that are more mechanical but no less fun, such as acrostics.

I ask the kids to volunteer a word or a name, the first one that comes to mind. One kid calls out "Jackass."

"Okay, I'm going to write this word in the traditional Chinese fashion, up and down."

J
a
c
k
a
s
s

"Someone give me a word, any word, that starts with *J*."
"Jackknife," one kid says.
"Yes, that's good. Any others?"
"Jupiter."
"Japan!"

"Jellybean!"

"Those are all terrific. Let's take jellybean." Which I do. "Okay, now what word begins with *A*?"

"Ambulance?"

"Great! Now let's put *jellybean* and *ambulance* together by adding some things before and after *jellybean*."

By now the kids are cracking up or staring in amazement at this peculiar teacher or racing ahead in their minds. In any case they are learning how to do an acrostic.

We finish the example at the board, and I read it aloud:

> The Jellybean drove an
> Ambulance to South
> Carolina because he was a
> Kook who
> Always
> Started
> Speeding wildly

Everyone's laughing.

"Pick a word of your own," I tell them—"and do an acrostic, just as we did at the board, putting in anything that pops into your mind, no matter how silly."

Onions

> July smells like
> Onions when it is
> Hot and
> Niagara Falls
> Runs dry because
> Onions clog the
> Immense
> Merging of the
> Entire
> Roto Rooter Company

(John Roimer)

Another writing method kids enjoy is collaborating as a class, dictating lines to someone at the board. This is also a good way to start with a class that hates writing, like one fourth grade group I taught. Here is their class collaboration:

Angels are workers of God
Angels are the shoeshiners of God
Does God wear shoes?
No, he's a spirit
He might wear spiritual shoes
He puts on his underwear
It's pink and white
He goes to New Jersey
There he visits his family
In his family are George Washington, Babe Ruth, Mister
    McGoo and Mister Boogie
They dance
Then God takes an elevator
Like Jack and the beanstalk
And he's a rocket
Going to the moon, to the sky, to outer space

In a more advanced fourth-grade class the kids chose part-
ners and wrote alternating lines. These fourth-graders had a
lot of experience writing poetry, which can be seen in this
sample that still makes me dizzy with envy:

What's Inside the Moon?

What's inside the moon?
    There's hot water inside.
What's the sky made of?
    It was made out of white snow.
If you cut the sun open what would you see?
    Terrible looking enemies.
When you write you look at your words have you thought of
    cutting open a letter to see what's inside?
    No. But if a person was crazy the answer would be yes.
What's inside colors?
    There's pink stars.
Where is the end of the universe?
    In back of the swimming pool.
How old is adventure?
    It is 60,00 years old.
Which color is older, black or white?
    Black because you can outline me.
        (Vivien Tuft and Fontessa Moore, P.S. 61, New York City)

Sometimes with younger kids I sit down at the class type-writer and wait for them to come over and start dictating to me. One second-grade class didn't need much encouragement. They rushed over to dictate:

Sneezes of Hair

In the middle of the night
A hand comes out and says, "Hiya, honey,"
And kisses her in the lips
And she makes him baldheaded and he says, "I'm bald!
    I'm bald!"
And he puts pepper on his head
And it sneezes up

It became so exciting, one kid climbed up on top of my head, searching for sneezes of hair, I guess.

At first, kindergartners were hard to teach because of their inability to write words or to concentrate very long, but I found them so much fun to be with that I usually let them look in my pockets, pull my beard, put toys on my shoes, etc. Then one day I enlisted the aid of five sixth-graders, good poets who had been writing for several years. I gave them some ideas for poems the kindergartners might like: "You know how your mother or father always says the same things. What do they say at your house? If your dog or cat or fish could talk English, what would they say? If a tree or a leaf or a mountain could talk, what would they say? A table? Imagine a talking table! A talking shoe? The moon talking! A glass of milk!" We broke into flying wedges, each sixth-grader in charge of three or four little kids. They worked much better with the sixth-graders than they had with me. Here are two poems dictated that day.

Poem

When a leaf drops it goes
tic, thoup, roasp,
wee wee weeee, ahhhhh

My Daddy Says

My Daddy says walk the dog
My Daddy says clean the cat
My Daddy says keep the tiger in the cage
My Daddy says brush your teeth
My Daddy says meow
My Daddy says wa wa wa Indian
My Daddy says eat the dog and leave the cat
My Daddy says ruf, ruf, ruf
My Daddy says feed the monkey bananas
My Daddy says I drive him bananas
My Daddy says don't get dirty
My Daddy says play it cool

I encourage kids to use my ideas in any way they like, even to the point of replacing them with their own ideas. One boy, San Lum Wong, newly arrived from China and just beginning to learn English, wrote the following poem when I asked his class to write Love Poems:

The Funny World

The world is funny. The earth is funny. The people is funny. Somebody in funny life. Somebody given a life change the funny. The magic is funny. The funny is magic. Oh, boy a funny funny money happy.

I defy you to write something in Chinese half as beautiful about love after three months of studying that language.

Sometimes a student will hand me a manuscript, something written at home in private. Such a poem was that of Liz Wolf, a seventh-grader.

I Kiss No Ass

I follow no footsteps because the ones I start to make I end
And I don't need your sun
'Cause I am my own sun, I can make light for myself, so I can
    see the light

I don't need your gentle fingertips because I have my own
    two hands
And I have no room for hassles
No time, I don't have any need for it and it doesn't have any
    need for me
You can use your army and shield to knock me down
But my feet are planted to the ground
You tell me to "kiss ass"
I want to say, "Don't they know I have a mind too,
I'm not stupid!"
But what I say is "I kiss *no* ass."

Once kids come to appreciate their own writing, they have
an improved, in fact a corrected, opinion of themselves, be-
cause one's language is as integral a part of one's self as an arm
or leg. By getting in touch with their creative imaginations—
which is sometimes a scary business, not a cutesy-pie world of
daffodils and little hills—they see more clearly into them-
selves, and this clarity gives them a sense of personal value.
Creativity is not something to be tacked on to the curriculum,
it's essential to growing and learning.

Educational administrators and classroom teachers are be-
ginning to see that imaginative writing is not just a "cultural
enrichment" to which they "expose" their kids. By having kids
indulge themselves in the wild and wacky world of the imagi-
nation, presto: schoolwork improves, school becomes a bit
more fun, and the printed word loses some of its tyranny.
When kids can look at books and articles and say, confidently,
"I write too," they are much less likely to acquiesce to the
printed word without question, less likely to become mindless
victims of mindless power.

Poetic Forms

As publications director of Teachers & Writers Collaborative, I edited their Handbook of Poetic Forms, *which now includes 77 entries by 19 poets. I wrote the eleven entries that follow. Our intended audience was high school students and college undergraduates.*

Acrostic
("uh-CROSS-tic")

The word *acrostic* comes from the Greek *acros* (outermost) and *stichos* (line of poetry). As a literary form, the basic acrostic is a poem in which the first letters of the lines, read downwards, form a word, phrase, or sentence. For example, in the following short acrostic, the vertical word is *our:*

> Open your mind to the
> Universe, and
> Run back home and get your lunch.
> > (Juan Lugo, seventh grade)

Some acrostics have the vertical word at the end of the lines, or in the middle. The *double acrostic* has two such vertical arrangements (either first and middle letters or first and last letters), the *triple acrostic* has all three (first letters, middle, and last). Here is what might be called a run-on double acrostic, with the last letter of each line capitalized only to make the example clearer:

> Many times I
> Yelled across the cosmoS
> Not knowing to whoM
> And/or what everlasting top bananA

Men had sought in faR
EternitY.

The acrostic originated in ancient times and was used in Greek, Hebrew, and Latin literature. Some of the biblical Psalms (in Hebrew) are acrostics. Authors who used acrostics include Plautus, Boccaccio, Chaucer, Ben Jonson, and Edgar Allan Poe, whose poem "A Valentine to ———— ————" uses the first letter of his beloved's name as the first letter of the first line, the second letter of her name as the second letter of the second line, and so on down, so that her name formed a diagonal from the top left to the bottom right of the poem.

Some ancient writers felt the acrostic had mystical power, but some later writers regarded the acrostic as an empty and trivial game. But any poetic form is trivialized by poor use, and the emptiness is the author's fault, not the form's. Besides, there is playfulness in all poetic forms.

Acrostics are easy to write. First, you write vertically the word or phrase, then go back and fill out the lines, using as many words as you like. Try it with your own name. The acrostic is good for developing mental and verbal agility, especially when written at top speed. It is interesting to turn a word or phrase on its side and see what spills out.

Bouts-Rimés
("boo re-MAY")

Bouts-rimés is French for "rhymed ends." A bouts-rimés poem is created by one person's making up a list of rhymed words and giving it to another person, who in turn writes the lines that end with those rhymes, in the same order in which they were given. For example, one person writes down *tanned, jump, fanned, lump, reading, lawn, misleading, yawn, yo-yo, death, no-no, breath, France,* and *pants* for another person to use as rhymes, as in:

Getting burnt, evaporated, bleached, or tanned
By the sun ain't no way to jump.
I'd rather plop in shadow, be fanned
By some geisha girl, and lay around like a proverbial lump.

144

I'm not that hot for so-called good reading;
I just crave a cool drink on a bluegreen lawn.
I mean, don't let me be misleading:
Where I'm at is sorta like the center of a yawn.

You know, excitement's like being a yo-yo—
I don't wanna beat the subject to death,
And it isn't that repetition ain't no no-no,
But the last thing I hope to be is out of breath.

So let somebody else go lost-generate all over France,
Or fly to the moon, discover Africa, some damn hotshot
    smartypants.

                                        (Jack Collom)

The weirder the list of rhymes, the more challenging it is to
make them make sense together and seem natural. On the
other hand, the author might want to create a poem that
doesn't make sense (see "Nonsense Verse"). Either way, the
bouts-rimés poem requires wit and mental agility.

Bout-rimés are said to have been invented by a seven-
teenth-century French poet named Dulot. They were very
popular throughout the eighteenth and nineteenth centuries,
when they were known in English as "crambo." In 1864 Alex-
andre Dumas, the author of *The Three Musketeers,* invited all
the poets of France to fill in the lines for a set of selected
rhymes. The next year he published the result: 350 poems by
as many poets, all with the exact same rhymes. Why not do the
same with a group of friends, a class, a school, a city?

Cento
("SEN-toe")

The word *cento* comes from the Latin word meaning "patch-
work," as in "patchwork quilt." The cento is a poem made
entirely of pieces from poems by other authors. Centos can be
rhymed or unrhymed, short or long. Here is one example by
John Ashbery:

Where, like a pillow on a bed
I come to pluck your berries harsh and crude
Where through the Golden Coast, and groves of orange and
 citron
And one clear call for me
My genial spirits fail
The desire of the moth for the star
When first the College Rolls receive his name.

Too happy, happy tree
Here, where men sit and hear each other groan.
Forget this rotten world, and unto thee
Go, for they call you, Shepherd, from the hill
And the eye travels down to Oxford's towers.

Calm was the day, and through the trembling air
Coffee and oranges in a sunny chair
And she also to use newfangleness . . .
Why cannot the Ear be closed to its own destruction?
Last noon beheld them full of lusty life,
Unaffected by "the march of events,"
Never until the mankind making
From harmony, from heavenly harmony
O death, I cover you over with roses and early lilies!
With loaded arms I come, pouring for you
Sunset and evening star
Where roses and white lilies grow.
Go, lovely rose,
This is no country for old men. The young
Midwinter spring is its own season
And a few lilies blow. They that have power to hurt, and will
 do none.
Looking as if she were alive, I call.
The vapours weep their burthen to the ground.
Obscurest night involved the sky
When Loie Fuller, with her Chinese veils
And many a nymph who wreathes her brow with sedge . . .
We have given our hearts away, a sordid boon!
In drear-nighted December
Ripe apples drop about my head
Who said: two vast and trunkless legs of stone
To throw that faint thin line upon the shore!

O well for the fisherman's boy!
Fra Pandolf's hand
Steady thy laden head across a brook . . .
With charm of earliest birds; pleasant the sun
Fills the shadows and windy places
Here in the long unlovely street.
Ah, sad and strange as in dark summer dawns
The freezing stream below.
To know the change and feel it . . .

At that far height, the cold thin atmosphere
Pressed her cold finger closer to her lips
Where the dead feet walked in.
She dwells with Beauty—Beauty that must die,
Or the car rattling o'er the stony street.

Centos go back at least as far as the second century. In the fifth century a cento was written on the life of Christ, with every line borrowed from the Greek poet Homer, whose work was created at least 900 years *before* Christ! Centos continued to be written up until the seventeenth century, often by churchmen, who could read Latin and therefore use the classics handed down from Roman times.

Using lines from other sources has been revived in the twentieth century. T. S. Eliot in *The Waste Land,* Ezra Pound in *The Cantos,* Ted Berrigan in *The Sonnets,* and many others have mixed borrowed lines with their own work, creating what might be called "collage" poems. But few modern poets have created true centos, poems made *entirely* of other poets' lines.

A good way to write a cento is to keep a notebook in which you collect lines that strike you. After you've accumulated a bunch, see if they can be arranged to make a new poem.

Another way is to examine the index of first lines in a poetry collection. Sometimes these indexes contain undiscovered centos, as in *An Anthology of New York Poets:*

Yes, they are alive, and can have those colors,
Yippee! she is shooting in the harbor! he is jumping
You approach me carrying a book
You are bright, tremendous, wow.

Most poetry anthologies have lots of lines beginning with the words *I, you, a,* and *the,* and in the index of first lines these tend to form ready-made centos.

Calligram
("CAL-ih-gram")

The word *calligram* comes from the French *calligramme,* itself derived from the Greek *calli* and *gramma,* which together mean "beautiful writing."

The French poet Guillaume Apollinaire was aware of this meaning when he invented the French form of the word and used it as the title of his book of poems *Calligrammes* (1918). In this book, he published poems that didn't look like poems: his calligrams had words and lines in new combinations and shapes. Some of the calligrams had a shape that related to their subject, as in "It's Raining" (fig. 3). This poem is about how the rain reminds the poet of his past: women, marvelous encounters, horses and the towns suggested by their neighing, and how the path of the raindrop suggests lines that bind us to the sky and our past. But notice how different the poem would look and feel if it were printed the way poems usually are:

It's raining women's voices as if they were dead even in
    memory
it's also raining you marvelous encounters of my life O
    droplets
and these rearing clouds start neighing an entire world of
    auricular cities
listen if it's raining while regret and disdain weep an ancient
    music
listen to the falling lines that bind you high and low

It's not the same, is it?

Apollinaire wrote quite a few of these poems whose shapes reflect their subjects, poems shaped like a valentine, a star, a pistol, the Eiffel Tower, a necktie, a carnation, and so on. In doing so, he was in a worldwide tradition that, in the West, goes back at least as far as the ancient Greeks, the tradition of

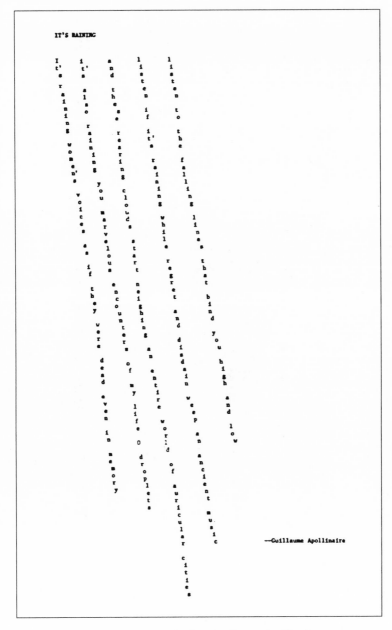

Fig. 3.   "It's Raining" by Guillaume Apollinaire

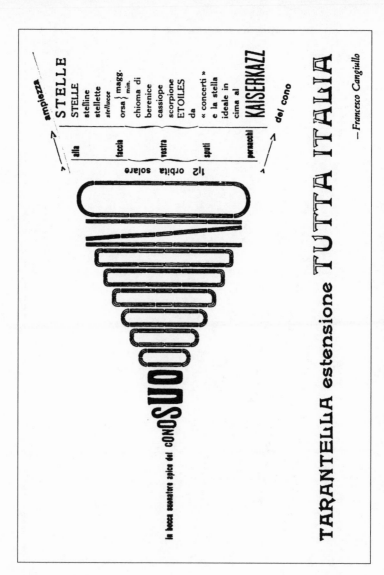

Fig. 4. Futurist calligram by Francesco Cangiullo

what is called "shaped poetry" or "pattern poetry." The English poet George Herbert (1593–1633) wrote two famous shaped poems, "Easter Wings" and "The Altar." In Lewis Carroll's *Alice's Adventures in Wonderland*, the mouse-tail might be considered a shaped poem.

Apollinaire's calligrams were a little different. Some of them were *not* in the shape of a particular thing: the lines were tilted around the page or with words in various sizes. In this, Apollinaire had been influenced by Stéphane Mallarmé's poem "A Throw of the Dice Will Never Abolish Chance," an astoundingly experimental poem published in 1897. But ultimately Apollinaire's calligrams came from his desire to invent a new kind of writing that he felt was necessary for expressing modern life.

At the same time, certain Italian and Russian artists and writers were experimenting along the same lines. They were known as the "Futurists." The Futurists were interested in "words set free." Figure 4 shows an example of a Futurist poem by Francesco Cangiullo (1916). In all these examples—shaped poems, calligrams, and Futurist words set free—the poem has taken a step towards turning itself into a visual artwork.

To write a calligram, you might first want to choose a shape that has a clear outline, such as a basketball or a window. Then fill in the shape with words and lines that come to you when you think about a particular basketball game or a particular window you look out of. Or you might want the words to be spoken by the basketball or the window. Remember, you can make the words any size, style, or color you want.

Epitaph
("EP-ih-taff")

An epitaph (from Greek, meaning "upon a tomb") is an inscription on a tomb, or writing suitable for that purpose.

The epitaph can be in prose or poetry; if poetry, it can be in any rhythmical pattern or none, rhymed or unrhymed. It should not be confused with the elegy, which, although often similar to the epitaph in subject and tone, is quite a bit longer.

Epitaphs range from the lofty to the coarse, from the sublimely serious to the shockingly hilarious. Some people have used satire to write their enemy's epitaph long *before* the enemy died.

The earliest examples of epitaphs, carved in stone, are from ancient Egypt. The Greeks and Romans became conscious of the epitaph as a literary form. Elegies were written throughout the Middle Ages, too, but it wasn't until the fifteenth century in England that the epitaph developed into an exceptionally high art.

Here are some examples of epitaphs.

> Underneath this sod lies John Round,
> Who was lost at sea, and never was found.

For a girl dead at seventeen:

> Sleep soft in dust until the Almighty will,
> Then rise, unchanged, and be an angel still.

*

> Here lies I
> Killed by a sky
> Rocket in my eye.

The following prose epitaph was written to commemorate a man who was scalded to death: "Sacred to the memory of our 'steamed friend." Most epitaphs, however, are sober and serious:

> *Epitaph on Elizabeth, L.H.*
>
> Wouldst thou hear what man can say
>   In a little? Reader, stay.
> Underneath this stone doth lie
>   As much beauty as could die;
> Which in life did harbor give
>   To more virtue than doth live.
> If at all she had a fault,
>   Leave it buried in this vault.
> One name was Elizabeth,
>   Th' other let it sleep with death;

Fitter, where it died to tell,
Than that it lived at all. Farewell.

(Ben Jonson)

Epithalamium
("ep-ih-thah-LAME-ee-oom")

The epithalamium is also called *epithalamion* and comes from a Greek word meaning "upon the bridal chamber." The epithalamium is a poem that celebrates a marriage.

Although there is no single fixed form for epithalamiums, they all have certain features: their subject is a particular marriage, they tell something about the wedding day, they praise the bride and groom, sometimes they tell about the bride and groom's past, they give blessings for the marriage and good wishes for its future happiness. Because the poet has lots of nice things to say about the bride and groom, and lots of blessings and good wishes to bestow, the epithalamium is not a short poem. It usually runs from around 40 to 400 lines. Some epithalamiums use rhyme and meter, others don't.

Traditional marriage songs have existed in most cultures, but the Greek poet Sappho, who lived around 600 B.C., is credited with having made the epithalamium a distinct literary form. In ancient times the epithalamium was sung by a chorus of boys and girls right outside the honeymooners' bedroom!

The Greeks and Romans wrote many epithalamiums, and the form was widely used in England, France, and Italy during the Renaissance. The first epithalamium in English was by Sir Philip Sidney, celebrating his own wedding (1580). Other notable examples are Edmund Spenser's "Epithalamium," John Donne's "Epithalamium Made at Lincoln's Inn," Robert Herrick's "An Epithalamie to Sir Thomas Southwell and his Ladie," Andrew Marvell's "Two Songs at the Marriage of the Lord Fauconberg and the Lady Mary Cromwell," Percy Shelley's "Fragment: Supposed to Be an Epithalamium of Francis Ravaillac and Charlotte Corday," and Alfred, Lord Tennyson's "To H.R.H. Princess Beatrice." Well-known twentieth-century examples are Guillaume Apollinaire's "Poem Read at the Wedding of André Salmon," and Frank O'Hara's "Poem Read at Joan Mitchell's."

If people you know are getting married and you want to give them something special, why not write them an epithalamium?

Imitation

For many centuries, philosophers and writers have discussed how art imitates life and how words imitate things. But, in talking about imitations here, we mean a poem that derives from a poem in another language and yet cannot be called a translation.

The poet Robert Lowell used the word this way in the title of his *Imitations,* a collection of poems based on his translations of poems by other poets. The traditional translator tries to make the translation as close an approximation to the original text as possible. Lowell, a poet, found that his translations took on a life of their own, a life that was different from that of the original text. What resulted were poems that couldn't really be called translations, nor could they be called original poems: they were halfway between. Lowell called them "imitations."

Other poets have been more casual in turning foreign language poems into English. For example, look at the following poem by Giuseppe Ungaretti. (It doesn't matter if you don't understand Italian. Just look at the words.)

Tutto Ho Perduto

Tutto ho perduto dell'infanzia
E non potrò mai più
Smemorarmi in un grido.

L'infanzia ho sotterrato
Nel fondo delle notti
E ora, spada invisibile,
Mi separa da tutto.

Di me rammento che esultavo amandoti,
Ed eccomi perduto
In infinito delle notti.

Disperazione che incessante aumenta
La vita non mi è più,
Arrestata in fondo alla gola,
Che una roccia di gridi.

This is a serious poem about losing one's childhood and feeling lost in an infinity of nights. Poet Ted Berrigan, who knew almost no Italian, turned this poem into:

Tooting My Horn on Duty

Tooting my horn on duty in the infantry
Made my name mud   P-U!
In the army I had nosebleeds

The infantry was distracting
It kindled up in my nose
An invisible odor
That hindered my toots

One day while on duty I rammed into a chestnut
And got blood all over my flute
Not to mention this nosebleed

I spat out so many teeth I knew it was an omen
The vitamins I took made me ill
Ten blood transfusions! It was almost all over
When two big rocks stopped the bleeding

This then was my unhappy childhood

Notice that Berrigan focused on certain words and ignored others. He took *tutto* (which means "all" or "everything" in Italian) and translated it as *tooting.* He took *infanzia* (infancy) and translated it as *infantry,* which probably made him see the word *army* in the last four letters of *smemorarmi.*

Berrigan's method is sometimes called intentional "mistranslation," that is, a translation error made on purpose. A more extreme type of mistranslation, in which the English version becomes more abstract and perhaps crazy, is when Pierre Reverdy's line "Un bonheur qui tremble encore est né" becomes "A bomb ear trembles in core of the knee."

If you understand even a little bit of a foreign language, try writing an imitation. You don't have to know any foreign language to do mistranslations. In either case, these kinds of poems are good to write because they teach you how to focus on the words, how they sound and fit together, and not to worry too much about the theme or subject. This is important, because ultimately poems are made not of feelings or ideas but of words.

Light Verse

Light verse is not a poetic form, it's a type of poetry. There are many varieties of it, including nonsense verse, limerick, parody, nursery rhymes, folk songs, occasional poems, alphabet poems, poems with lots of word play, epigrams, and what is called *vers de société* (French for "social verse"). *Vers de société* is brief, sophisticated, graceful, and witty poetry usually about social relationships and conventions. Like all light verse, *vers de société* expects its readers to understand it and find it agreeable to their way of looking at things. The poet W. H. Auden described light verse as "poetry which is simple, clear, and gay." In other words, it is not the poetry of an alienated, gloomy person who writes things that no one else can understand.

Light verse was popular in Greek and Latin classical literature. Many writers (including some who are thought of only as "serious" writers) have written light verse: among them, Aristophanes, Shakespeare, Goethe, Milton, Jonson, Pope, Lewis Carroll, T. S. Eliot, and Ogden Nash.

Because light verse can be written in so many different ways, it's impossible to give brief advice on how to write it, and it's misleading to provide only an example or two. The best way to learn more about it is to read lots of it, beginning, perhaps, with *The Oxford Book of Light Verse.*

Nonsense Verse

Nonsense verse is poetry that doesn't make sense, but it isn't just formless gibberish. For example,

```
eyu.;w/ k.l ..yvv;uo:-
rt"dxk,'qqq
d
l.shr,)
fpb
```

is not an example of nonsense verse, whereas the following is:

A *Tetrastich in the Lanternish Language*

Briszmarg dalgotbrick nubstzne zos,
Isquebsz prusq: albok crinqs zacbac.
Mizbe dilbarskz morp nipp stancz bos,
Strombtz, Panurge, walmap quost gruszbac.

(François Rabelais)

Rabelais's lines are of a regular length, the punctuation is consistent, and the lines rhyme. It gives us the feeling that if we only understood Lanternish we would understand the poem. That's the trick: Lanternish is a language complete with its own rules, but we will never be able to understand it because it is a made-up language. True nonsense verse gives us the feeling that it comes from a world different from ours, a world with its own rules, as in this anonymous nonsense poem:

There was a man of Thessaly,
    And he was wondrous wise,
He jumped into a bramble bush
    And scratched out both his eyes.
And when he saw his eyes were out,
    With all his might and main
He jumped into another bush
    And scratched them in again.

Although this poem is in clear English, its logic is alien. Like the Lanternish, however, it is perfectly consistent. We know it doesn't make sense, but we delight in it.

All good nonsense verse tickles the mind and gives delight. The most quoted nonsense verses are probably certain nursery rhymes and anonymous folk poetry, such as

What's your name?
Puddin Tane.
Ask me again
And I'll tell you the same.

Perhaps the most famous printed nonsense poem is Lewis Carroll's "The Jabberwocky." Other good writers of nonsense verse are Edward Lear, Walter de la Mare, Christian Morgenstern, and Stevie Smith.

Good nonsense verse is surprisingly hard to write. It requires that the author keep the poem consistent while at the same time letting it be crazy. It's not hard to be consistent, and it's not hard to write crazily, but it's hard to do both at the same time and have the result be light, tantalizing, and satisfying. Also, there's a fine line between good nonsense and plain silliness.

As with most poetic forms, one of the best ways to learn to write it is to read lots of it. You'll be more attracted to some types of nonsense verse than to others; they'll seem more natural to you. These are the first ones to try writing yourself. Then, as you write, don't worry about the result. Instead, let yourself get all the way into the world of the poem. To test your poem, read it to children and see what they think of it.

Ottava Rima
("o-TAH-vah REE-ma")

Ottava rima (from Italian, meaning roughly "rhyme in eights") is a stanza of eight lines that rhyme *ababab cc*. In English the lines follow the rhythmical pattern of iambic pentameter. Here's a contemporary example of a stanza in ottava rima:

> One night in Venice, near the Grand Canal,
> A lovely girl was sitting by her stoop.
> Sixteen years old, Elizabeth Gedall,
> When, suddenly, a giant ice-cream scoop
> Descended from the clouded blue corral
> Of heaven and scooped her skyward with a loop—
> The-loopy motion, which the gods of Venice
> Saw, and, enraged, they left off cosmic tennis. . . .
> (From Kenneth Koch, *The Duplications*)

Ottava rima had been used in thirteenth-century Italian religious verse, but in the next century the Italian poet Giovanni Boccaccio adapted it for more purely artistic purposes to tell long and interesting stories. In the early sixteenth century, Ludovico Ariosto used ottava rima in his epic poem *Orlando Furioso* (Frenzied Roland), a wonderfully long and rich work that mixes the comic and the serious, story and commentary, history and fantasies that include flying horses, knights, and maidens, and a trip to the moon.

Other poets of the Renaissance—Italian, Spanish, Portuguese, and English—also used ottava rima, but after Ariosto the next great master of the form was the English poet George Gordon, better known as Lord Byron. Byron's witty mind and gift of gab found ottava rima to be the perfect form for his *Don Juan*. The best-known modern practitioner of ottava rima is Kenneth Koch, who used it in his *Ko, or a Season on Earth* and *The Duplications*.

Some poets have used ottava rima for poems shorter than epics, but ottava rima is associated with long poems because its most famous examples have been long: *Orlando Furioso* (38,736 lines) and *Don Juan* (15,784 lines). Like most epics, these poems are divided into cantos, the way a novel is usually divided into chapters. The first six lines of each stanza, rhyming *ababab,* seem to encourage the unwinding of the imagination, and the last two lines, rhyming *cc,* often give it a short pause to rest before continuing. It's a very comfortable form that allows the story to plunge straight ahead, digress, go off on a tangent, or switch to another thread of the plot, ranging freely through space and time. The best way to get a feel for ottava rima is to immerse yourself in reading it in great long stretches (without worrying too much about the parts you don't understand). Then get lots of paper and start writing a story that has the possibility of going on for a long time.

Pantoum
("pan-TOOM")

Pantoum is the Western word for the Malayan *pantun,* a poetic form that first appeared in the fifteenth century, in Malayan literature. It existed orally before then. Making up pantoums was highly popular, and Malayans knew the most famous ones by heart.

The Western version of the pantoum is a poem of indefinite length made up of stanzas whose four lines are repeated in a pattern: lines 2 and 4 of each stanza are repeated as lines 1 and 3 of the next stanza, and so on, as shown here:

    ——————————————————— (line 1)
    ——————————————————— (line 2)
    ——————————————————— (line 3)
    ——————————————————— (line 4)

    ——————————————————— (line 5—same as line 2)
    ——————————————————— (line 6)
    ——————————————————— (line 7—same as line 4)
    ——————————————————— (line 8)

    ——————————————————— (line 9—same as line 6)
    ——————————————————— (line 10)
    ——————————————————— (line 11—same as line 8)
    ——————————————————— (line 12)

And so on.

Sometimes the final stanza has a neat twist: although its first and third lines are as usual the same as the second and fourth lines in the stanza above it, its second and fourth lines are the same as the third and first lines of the very first stanza. This way, every line in the poem is used twice, and the first line of the poem is the same as the last. Rhyme is optional. It all sounds complicated, but, if you look at this example, you'll see that our basic pantoum form is quite easy:

> Because birds are gliding across your brain,
> I rise into the shadows
> And the mist is rolling in
> Because my breath is rolling out.
>
> I rise into the shadows
> Like a pond that went to sleep:
> Because my breath is rolling out
> You hear doorbells in the woods.

Like a pond that went to sleep
And woke up inside a dream,
You hear doorbells in the woods
Though the woods are in the dream

And woke up inside a dream!
Although the air is filled with blue and white clouds,
Though the woods are in the dream,
A good idea can smell like pine trees.

Although the air is filled with blue and white clouds,
I am filled with ideas about dreams.
A good idea can smell like pine trees
And a dream can grow like a cloud.

I am filled with ideas about dreams.
The stars don't know what they mean
And a dream can grow like a cloud:
You can't explain this bigness.

The stars don't know what they mean
And the mist is rolling in.
You can't explain this bigness
Because birds are gliding across your brain.

The pantoum was first described in the West by Victor Hugo, poet and author of *The Hunchback of Notre Dame,* in 1829. Other French poets then wrote pantoums: Théodore de Banville, Louisa Siefert, Leconte de Lisle, Théophile Gautier, and, with considerable variation, Charles Baudelaire. The pantoum was taken up in England in the late nineteenth century, most notably by Austin Dobson in his "In Town" and James Brander Matthews in his "En Route."

The pantoum was used very little in America until it was revitalized by John Ashbery in his book *Some Trees* (1956); his "Pantoum," a variation on the basic pantoum form, inspired a group of young New York poets to write pantoums of their own and to teach pantoum writing to their students.

Part of the pleasure of the pantoum is the way its recurring lines gently and hypnotically twine in and out of one another, and the way they surprise us when they fit together in unexpected ways.

Other Voices

Silent reading is tricky: it isn't always silent. In the first place, some people "move their lips," even going so far as to whisper the words. When I was a child, lip moving was associated with the way old people read. My grandfather used to sit in his easy chair, reading the newspaper, unaware that a steady stream of subtle hissing was issuing from his lips.

A more subtle and interesting aspect of silent reading occurs when readers keep their lips still but "hear" in their heads the words on the page. This silent hearing is called "subvocalization." Reading teachers are now taught to discourage both lip moving and subvocalization. (My teachers never even brought up the idea of subvocalization.) Like lip moving, subvocalization is frowned upon because it reduces reading speed: you can't hear words as quickly as you can see them.

But, may I ask, what's the hurry? I *like* subvocalization. The books I most enjoy reading are those that have a definite "voice," a voice provided by the author. What this means is that the style is so distinct that we're able to communicate with a specific, real person: the author.

The author does this by writing either in the first person or the third person, as in these examples:

I woke up around 7 and lay in bed thinking about getting up. After an hour I did finally manage to swing my feet over the side of the bed and to place them flat on the cold marble floor.

He woke up around 7 and lay in bed thinking about getting up. After about an hour he did finally manage to swing his feet

"Other Voices" is adapted from *Creative Reading* (National Council of Teachers of English, 1997).

over the side of the bed and to place them flat on the cold marble floor.

The difference in wording—a few changes of pronouns—is very slight, but its effect on the tone is larger. The two examples "feel" different from one another.

Some types of books lend themselves readily to either first- or third-person treatment. Autobiographies and nonfiction travel books are two of the simplest, most direct uses of the first person. (Gertrude Stein, always exceptional, wrote somebody else's autobiography: *The Autobiography of Alice B. Toklas.*) But, as we saw in the previous chapter, the first person is not always so cut and dried. In fiction, for instance, the "I" may not be the author; it might be a character created by the author to tell the story: the *narrator*. Although we usually assume a bond of trust between the author and us, we cannot make such an assumption between the narrator and us. Sometimes the narrator tells the story in a self-serving way, or simply lies. And what if the narrator turns out to be a lunatic? We cannot blame the author for the mental or moral condition of the narrator, any more than we can blame any other character for such conditions.

The voice in third-person writing is less thorny. Here it may be assumed to be that of the author, with no tricky intermediary. However, the voice can have great range, from the statistical report that is highly objective to the novel whose author is so engaged in the story that he or she cannot resist interrupting it to comment, praise, or blame.

Although most books are cast in essentially either one mode or the other, some have internal variations. Nonfiction in the third person often is interspersed with quotations in the first person. Some first-person novels might be more aptly called first-people novels: different chapters are narrated by different characters. Such novels often use those characters' names as the chapter title ("Chapter 1: Bill. Chapter 2: Frederika"). In both these variations, though, the reader knows at all times who is speaking.

This does not hold true for certain modern works. In Joyce's *Finnegans Wake,* we are hard pressed to say who is speaking. Is it the author? A character? Or characters? The same goes for Eliot's *Waste Land,* Ashbery's poem "The Skaters," and Ted Berrigan's *Sonnets.* In a burst of immodesty, I'll add my own work to this group, a novel called *Antlers in the Treetops,* written in collaboration with Tom Veitch. The voice in *Antlers* shifts every few paragraphs, from author(s) to one character, then another, then to an entirely different author or set of authors, requiring the reader to invent a new voice every few paragraphs.

For, if we become involved with a text, we tend to invent a voice to hear it in. We invite what we assume is an appropriate tone of voice, such as the laconic, manly voice of Hemingway in the Nick Adams stories, the exquisite, sometimes peevish voice of Sei Shonagon in her *Pillow Book,* the sophisticated, subtly modulated voice of Henry James in *The Golden Bowl,* the robust voice of Whitman in *Leaves of Grass,* the angular and deceptively quiet voice of Emily Dickinson in her poems. Sometimes when I read such authors, I "hear" these voices quite clearly. This subvocalization has a bonding effect on me and the words. That it causes me to read slower is anything but a drawback, it is exactly what I want! I love the feeling that the author is speaking to me, as if he or she were in the room with me. This is particularly exciting if the author lived far away and long ago.

Inventing these voices can be, I admit, shaky business. If you misinterpret the material, you intensify the error by inventing a voice based on the misinterpretation. Inventing the voices of writers from other cultures can be particularly risky. For some, the temptation, when reading Chinese poetry, might be to "hear" it as if its authors were essentially one big lyrical Charlie Chan; that is, our cultural stereotypes can force widely different works into one mold. In doing so, we take the work one step farther away from the original, just as the translation into English did, and the farther away we get from the origin, the less of its character remains.

Work that has little character in the first place is immune to such misinterpretation. Dry, official, toneless writing is dry, official, and toneless in translation, and it has the same "voice" as that which issues from the mouths of so many public and private officials. These people speak unnaturally because their speech imitates, and rather poorly, at that, formal, written language. When our education does not succeed in teaching us to think in complex structures, we cannot speak in complex structures either. We cannot utter long, grammatically complex (and correct) sentences; we cannot arrange our thoughts into logical groups; and we cannot order such groups into a cohesive whole. To compensate, we use technical and official jargon, fashionable "buzz" words, and important-sounding latinisms. Alas, such a way of speaking precipitates into the culture, like acid rain. Inventing accurate voices for the texts written by such people can hardly be called invention; it is, rather, an exercise in memory. In public, the speaker talks like bad writing, thinks like bad writing, and in private creates more bad writing; the reader immediately recognizes this universal voice, so unmistakable on the page. The whole chain of thinking, writing, and reading not only has no originality, but also has no connection with the natural voice (in both senses of the word). If only some of these people who make speeches and give news conferences would talk to us the way they talk (we assume) at home! If we cannot have clear public speech of intellectual character, let us have at least a little down-home authenticity.

But we have little of that. So what are we to do with such dull material? Well, we can simply not read it.

Or we can try *voice substitution*. It's an old technique used by comedians but never, so far as I know, applied to reading. All you have to do is substitute a voice different from that of the text. For example, when reading the text of a dictator, imagine it being delivered by Donald Duck. If the text of a "tobacco industry spokesman" bores you, imagine it in the voice of a professional wrestler. If you are driven up the wall by the platitudes of a school commencement address, imagine it being delivered in the voice of Marlene Dietrich or Hattie McDaniel.

This is similar to a method used by comic musician Spike Jones. The typical Spike Jones song begins with soothing, romantic material, as in "Cocktails for Two":

> Oh what delight to
> Be given the right to
> Be carefree and gay once again,
> No longer slinking
> Respectably drinking

> Like civilized ladies and men,
> No longer need we miss
> A charming scene like this:
> In some secluded rendez-vous. . . .

Suddenly a maniacal voice shrieks "Whoopee!," a police whistle sounds, a gun fires, and the music goes completely wild. The vocalist maintains his suavity but is constantly undercut with burlesque sound effects (his crooning of "And we'll enjoy a cigarette" is followed by an emphysemic cough). This undercutting radically transforms the original material. It's a shame more young people don't know about Spike Jones; he is a delightful way to learn about broad parody and burlesque.

Jones was the master of his style, but his range was narrow. You might want to try more subtle transformations. In any case, combine whatever voice with whatever material you wish, keeping in mind that the greater the difference between voice and text, the more bizarre (and sometimes comic) the effect.

A similar set of techniques can be applied to reading good writing. Let's say you are hooked on the crime novels of Elmore Leonard. Let's also say you have a favorite uncle who used to run numbers. Why not imagine his voice reading Elmore Leonard to you? That's what the companies that produce spoken arts tapes and CDs do: they try to match up the voice with the material. They paired off Irish actress Siobhan McKenna and James Joyce's writing; they hired Jay Silverheels (who played Tonto in the Lone Ranger radio programs and movies) to read native American poems and tales; they got spooky Vincent Price to read the horror tales of Edgar Allan Poe. You can use anyone's voice—a famous person's or a friend's—as the voice of the book.

When, after many attempts, I finally broke the Proust barrier and got so far into *Remembrance of Things Past* that I never wanted to get out, I found that the book provided its own voice for me to hear, the voice of Marcel, the narrator. It was a cultured, sensitive voice. One afternoon a friend came by for a nice, long chat. That night, when I resumed my reading, I heard *his* voice instead of Marcel's, as I recorded in a poem:

I am aware of the volume,
the pages, their size and color
and their texture, with edges
and their words set in blocks
surrounded with margins,
And I am aware too of the meaning
of the words and sentences,
the majestic flotilla of the paragraphs
in the flow of the story—I recognize
the characters and remember them
from page to page, and I note
the art of the writing and the quality
of the author's mind, and I see him
writing his book, the words of which
I hear being read aloud to me
by a friend, whom I saw today
and who had stayed in my mind,
offering, while there, to perform
this service.

Literal oil flowed across

Then I went on reading

Given my friend's personality, the substitution worked fine. My friend became "Marcel" for that night. The next day, I went back to using the original Marcel voice, refreshed by the respite from it.

The experience of hearing a friend's voice in my head was more frequent when I was in my early twenties. In those days I would often spend 10 or 12 hours with Ted Berrigan, the poet, who was a Rabelaisian conversationalist with a highly distinct way of talking. Each time we parted, his voice continued to reverberate in my head. Everything I read I heard in his voice. Everything I said sounded as if he were saying it. Of course, the remembered voice "decayed" over the next few days, and I returned to a more various way of hearing. (Every time I see the word *various,* though, I hear a little of Frank O'Hara, who used the word *variously* so beautifully in one of his poems, and of Lionel Trilling, who used it frequently in his lectures.) People who are young enough to be impressionable but old enough to do good imitations are prime candidates for learning how to assimilate voices, store them, and use them in their reading. It also helps, of course, to live in a culturally diverse society, although I suppose that anyone with a television set has access to a wide variety of voices.

We should not overlook the possibility of applying *incongruous* voices to good writing. When the poetry of Wallace Stevens starts to sound overintellectualized, I sometimes "hear" it in the voice of a Southern redneck. T. S. Eliot's poetry is particularly delightful when heard in a strong Oklahoma accent ("Aprul eh-is thuh croolist munth"). I like to imagine how William Carlos Williams's poems—so American—would sound in an Italian accent. I would like to be able to "hear" an Eskimo cast perform *A Midsummer Night's Dream,* a Jamaican read *Paradise Lost.* We can also combine authors in any number of ways; we can, for instance, imagine T. S. Eliot in the unforgettable voice of Truman Capote, or vice versa. Such unusual pairings result in what amounts to burlesque, but frequently in the burlesque you see clearly an aspect of the writer's work that was previously too familiar to be noticed. The forest and the trees are separated.

Our own voices are the most familiar of all. That is to say, when we speak we are so accustomed to hearing ourselves that we cease to notice how we sound, unless there are unusual circumstances, such as a "frog in the throat" or a tape recording. Most people, hearing themselves on tape for the first time, ask, "Is *that* me? Do I really sound like that?" The reason the voice on the tape sounds different is that we are receiving the sound waves solely from outside our heads, whereas when we speak, we hear the sound from both inside and outside our heads. The new experience of hearing ourselves only from the outside makes most of us feel that we sound horrible, partly because we are distressed to find that we aren't what we had always thought we were, partly because we become self-conscious when attention—like a camera—is directed on us.

In learning to read better and more creatively, however, attention to self is exactly what is called for. You might ask yourself:

- Do I subvocalize?
- Do I subvocalize sometimes or always? Does the subvocalized voice flicker in and out?
- Do I subvocalize when it isn't necessary (as in reading the contents listing on a food can)?
- Do I subvocalize in different voices? If so, how do I arrive at those voices?
- Do I subvocalize in only one voice? What or whose voice is it?

Many people use a combination of these subvocalizations. They don't subvocalize single words (like STOP on a street sign) or brief phrases; nor do they subvocalize certain types of material, such as scientific and mathematical data, lists of facts, flat nonfiction, and the like. They do subvocalize some poetry (where the sound can be crucial to the whole experience of the work) and fiction (they might hear British novels in an English accent, for instance). But, by and large, the single most common voice used in subvocalization seems to be a ghost version of one's own speaking voice. This voice is the old reliable of voices, the one that arises naturally when needed, when no other voices suggest themselves. (It is also the one we hear when we think in words.) So in a sense, when we use our own voice for subvocalization, we are not simply reading to ourselves, we are appropriating the text, modeling it to our own tone, reshaping its emotional contours. Without changing the words, we are rewriting the text.

This discussion of voice in reading would be incomplete without mention of a relatively recent phenomenon: the availability of the author's actual voice. In the past 40 years, there has been a tremendous increase in the number of live performances and recordings by authors reading their own work.

Before the 1950s relatively few American authors read their work to large groups in public; only one poet comes readily to mind: Vachel Lindsay. Coffeehouse poetry readings were not uncommon in Greenwich Village and the Lower East Side of New York in the 1920s and 1930s, but their audiences were small and localized. Most of the poetry readings in the 1940s and early 1950s were by "distinguished" older poets—mostly men, although Gertrude Stein was an exception—who were invited to read their poetry or perhaps deliver a talk at a university. The big breakthrough occurred when Dylan Thomas toured America. Thomas's musical and dramatic intonations swept listeners off their feet; you can get some idea of the distinctive power of his voice by listening to any of the recordings still readily available. I remember hearing his recording of "Fern Hill" when I was in high school. I had read the poem before, but I wasn't prepared for the great lyrical blast of his voice. It sent me back to the printed page, and, when I got there and silently read the poem again, I could hear this voice "singing" it to me. To this day I subvocalize Dylan Thomas's voice when reading his work.

His voice is congruent with his work, as is Wallace Stevens's, Edna St. Vincent Millay's, Allen Ginsberg's, and those of many others. Other voices come as surprises. I read John Ashbery's early work for several years before hearing him read, and I subvocalized a voice for it, a voice something like John Wayne's. Ashbery's real voice came as a shock. It seemed—partly as a result of my expectations—rather nasal. Later I adjusted to his voice, which after all was not so bad and which blended perfectly with his new work, "perfectly" because in fact I was unable to read it without hearing his voice.

Did I understand his work any better, then? Some might argue that my original fantasy (the John Wayne voice) was, in fact, a more accurate representation of what has been called Ashbery's status as an "executive" poet. Is there always an advantage—or any advantage—in being acquainted with the author's speaking voice?

After listening to hundreds and hundreds of writers read their work, I've come to the conclusion that in some cases it helps, in some cases it doesn't. Some good writers read their own work poorly, making you wish you had stayed home with your own fantasy of the voice. Some writers who seem good read their work in such a way that you realize, hearing them, that their work isn't very good after all; its faults are revealed by the glare of public presentation. Other writers, whose work sometimes seems difficult on the page, come through with perfect clarity when they read it aloud. Here I'm thinking particularly of poets Kenneth Koch and Edwin Denby. Koch's gentle irony is perfectly clear and appropriate, as are Denby's shifting tones of everyday speech. When one goes back to their work on the page, the writing remains forever clarified. When hearing an author read, though, it's important to keep in mind that reading styles change, just as literary styles do. We shouldn't be disconcerted, for example, by the "old-fashioned" voice of "modernist" Ezra Pound.

The great opportunity we as readers have—with multitudes of public readings, tapes, and records now available—is to be able to invite not only an author's work into our minds but his or her voice as well. We have the opportunity of measuring the author's voice against whatever voice we had created for that author and, from there, of pondering the relative qualities of both. From this we move toward a greater understanding of what the work is (or isn't).

Here are some other ways to experiment with reading aloud:

1. *Duets:* one person reads silently, while another person reads a different text aloud. What effect does this have on the silent reader? How does the selection of material change the effect? Alternative: have both read different texts aloud.

2. *Choral readings:* a large group of people—a classroomful, for instance—simultaneously read different texts, creating a sort of sound environment. This can be orchestrated, to make it resemble the general hum of conversation in a restaurant, theater, or sports arena; to make it harmonious (as in a round such as "Row, Row, Row Your Boat"); to make it euphonious (perhaps creating an abstraction using a text with similar vowel and/or consonant sounds); to make it chaotic, with everyone reading completely different texts, either whispered or shouted.

A variation of choral reading is to have a group read in unison a text that is identical except for, say, its nouns. (Such a text can easily be prepared by having each person fill in the blanks.) What effect does such a reading have on the feel of the text? This exercise is not unlike the singing of "Happy Birthday to You," when everyone is in unison except when it comes to the name of the birthday person, who, it often turns out, is called by several different names. When the group momentarily divides at that point, the song always gets a little shaky.

Another option is to create word environments. Have the group simultaneously read aloud words that suggest:

- the ocean (*water, waves, whitecaps, splash, glug, crash, shhhh, whoosh*, etc.)
- the desert (*sand, palm tree, hot, dry, lizard, thirsty, sun, gasp*, etc.)
- night (*cool, dark, quiet, crickets, moon, stars, sleep*, etc.)
- the woods (*trees, green, wind, leaves, crunch, quiet, buzz, calm, alone*, etc.)

A variation of these word scenes is to combine words and sounds, as in:

- an orchestra, in which the *sounds* of the instruments are supported by a *basso continuo* of sentences of words *about* music
- a barnyard or zoo, in which animal sounds are mixed with words about animals
- a factory, with whistles, chugs, booms, and clicks mixed with words about manufacturing.

These exercises are fun in themselves, but they also set us to thinking about how to read aloud material that might be considered unreadable. How, for instance, would you read aloud what the man is saying here?

Fig. 5. Cussing man

The picture of the cussing man is a clue that makes the typographical symbols (in the speech balloon) into international symbols. Readers in Martinique or the Philippines or Albania would be able to "read" what he is saying.

How would you read the semicolon in Ron Loewinsohn's poem (fig. 6)? Obviously, the poet has created this poem more as a treat for the eye than for the ear, which is partly why it's challenging to try to figure out a good way to read it aloud.

SEMICOLON; for Philip Whalen

Semicolon   ;   like the head & forearm of a man swimming, the arm in foreshortened perspective, his head looking away   ;   his mouth's open in exaggerated O inhaling on the other side, his wrist's bent just about to re-enter the surf   ;   water dripping from the fingertips   ;   semicolon

Or a whole row of them

; ;

swimming off to Catalina

Fig. 6.   Ron Loewinsohn poem

Take a look at the poem in figure 7 by Paul de Vree. At first, it looks like a bunch of random letters and parentheses thrown up into the air, but if you look at it for a moment you'll notice that the letters are those of the title of a famous song, with something else thrown in. How would you read this poem aloud? I think I'd have four or five friends read it with me. I'd have everyone read or sing the words, out of synch, and perhaps with fluttery voices, since the parentheses remind me of birds fluttering around in the airy springtime Paris sky.

Another exercise is called *megaphone.* As you read any text aloud, get louder and louder, then softer and softer, then louder again, then softer again, and so on. Read so the change in volume has nothing to do with the text's content.

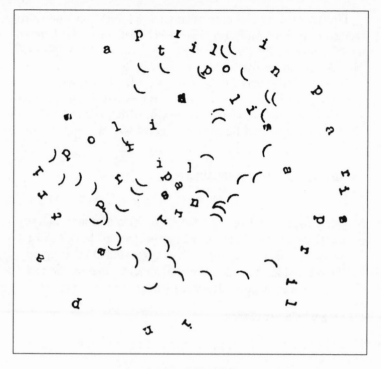

Fig. 7. Paul de Vree poem

There are several variations on *megaphone,* based on pitch. As you read aloud, start with your voice pitched low and have it gradually go up as high as it can, then back down, and so on.

Or have a pitch "twist" on each word, so that the voice rises on each word:

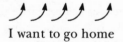

I want to go home

or falls on each:

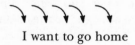

I want to go home

or alternates, one word with a rising twist, the next with a falling:

I want to go home

or with no change at all—a monotone:

I want to go home.

It's easier to read in a monotone if you imagine you're a robot or if you simulate a computer-generated voice. Intentionally reading in a monotone is particularly helpful for children whose oral reading tends to be toneless; the exaggerated monotone makes them realize that there is such a thing as tone and that reading aloud sounds so much better when it has tone, the way ordinary speech does.

Another voice skill valuable for reading is totally silent: listening. Listening is a form of reading, insofar as we "listen" to the words of what we read.

Try the following exercise. Close your eyes and open your ears: that is, focus your attention on what you hear. Keep listening until you think you've heard everything there is to hear at the moment, sounds in the far distance, sounds up close (such as that of your own breathing). If there are voices around you, so much the better. Notice how you immediately become more aware of all these sounds.

Here's another listening exercise. Ask a friend to talk with you while your eyes are closed. Pay close attention to every word your friend says, not just to the gist of them. Notice the tone, volume, and pace, and check to see if the words come in complete sentences or in little fragments. Then have your friend close his or her eyes too and continue the conversation. After a while, do you notice that you feel closer to your friend? Such a feeling of closeness occurs whenever we really listen to the other person, undistracted by other sounds, including those of our own thoughts. We interlock with our friend's words, and, in that sense, we show respect. We show that we feel that our friend's words are worthy of close attention.

Reading teachers, especially those in "whole language" classrooms, have become more aware of the importance of listening. Discussing the reading abilities of the deaf and the blind, Jeanne Chall says:

> Common sense tells us that the deaf would be the better readers because they can see the print. Yet the blind are the better readers. This happens because reading is closer to hearing than to seeing.

Good teachers consider listening an active skill that must be practiced and developed, especially in light of the passive hearing most children grow up with, sitting in front of the television, which, after all, is primarily a visual medium, one whose words (and music) are often not worth listening to anyway. But even those who grow up without television need to maintain their listening power, to overcome their natural tendency toward aural numbness. And, if one wants to read more creatively, the ability to listen carefully and continuously is even more crucial.

Finally, here are two exercises, for one person.

1. Pick any book and alternate reading silently and orally from it, alternating words, phrases, or sentences (the larger the syntactical unit, the easier the exercise).
2. How slowly can you read aloud and still retain the meaning of a sentence? Try reading any text aloud, slower and slower, until you're saying it word by word. After you say a word, keep your eyes on it; don't peek ahead to the next one. When you've really slowed down to, say, one word per 10 seconds, notice what your mind does in the silent intervals.

After doing any of the exercises in this essay, you'll find that your normal reading has become smoother, easier, and clearer.